My First Encyclopedia

First published 1982, 1983, 1984 by
MacDonald & Co (Publishers) Ltd
This edition specially produced
for CEEPI/Dealerfield Ltd, 1988.

a member of Maxwell Pergamon Publishing
Corporation plc

ISBN 0907305-17-2

Printed by NEW INTERLITHO, ITALY

Factual Advisers
Alistair Ross
Former ILEA advisory teacher on History and
Social Services
John Tranter
Centre for Life Studies (ILEA), Zoological
Gardens, Regents Park, London
Eileen Harries
Adviser for Humanities, London Borough of
Merton
Ian Bain
Editor, the Geographical Magazine
Dr David George
British Museum (Natural History)
Michael Boorer
Education Department, Zoological Society of
London, Regents Park, London
Andrew Nahun
a curator at the Science Museum, London

Reading Consultant
Geoffrey Ivimey
Department of Child Development and
Educational Psychology, University of
London

Designer
Ewing Paddock Associates

Teacher Panel
Penny Anderson
Geoffrey Barber
Susan Batten
Tim Firth
Penny French
Sue Frolish
Stephen Harley
David Hyams
Charmiàn Masterton
Lynn McCoombe
Ann Merriman
Cathy Phillips
David Rowbotham
Eduardo Zaccagnini de Ory

My First Encyclopedia

CAXTON

Contents

Me and You

Joanna Howard

About this chapter

There are four different animals in this picture
of the world. They live in different places.
What would happen if they changed places?
A crocodile is suited to jungle heat and water.
Could it live on the ice?
Could a polar bear live in the jungle?

One of the animals can live all over the world
– in the desert, the jungle or on the ice.
That animal is called a human. It is you and me
and all the other people in the world.
This chapter is about us and what we need to live.

Do you want to go into space? What would you need
to take with you to stay alive?

This pack helps the astronaut move in space. It also contains oxygen.

You need air, water and food to stay alive.
You also need clothes, a place to shelter and other people.
Have these astronauts got all of these things?

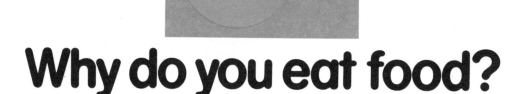

Why do you eat food?

How many times a day do you eat? Why do you eat?
You must eat because your body needs food all day.

We get food from plants and animals. The children
below are all eating a good meal. Can you name
what they are eating? Which plants and animals
does their food come from?

**What is your favourite meal?
Where do you think these
children come from?**

Food helps you grow. Food helps cuts and bruises heal. Food helps you keep well and gives you energy. You use energy to move and keep your body working, even when you sleep. A good meal has the different foods you need for this. People in some countries do not get enough food. Why do you think this is?

Everyone has favourite foods. What foods do grown-ups tell you are good for you? Do you like them? Other people may hate your favourite food.

Can your favourite food be bad for you? Yes, but only if you eat too much of it. You need to eat lots of different foods without too much of one thing. Even carrots, which are very good for you, could be bad for you if you ate too many.

Too many sweets or too much sugar make it easy for your teeth to rot.

This boy has not had enough of the foods that help bones to grow strong and straight.

People eat these animals in different countries. Some people would be disgusted to eat some of them.

Why you need water

Your outside may be dry, but your inside is wet.
Your body is made from lots of water. Every bit
of your body needs water to work.
You can live for only a few days without water
before your body stops working and you die.
You can live longer without food.

Water comes out of you when you go to the lavatory
and when you sweat. Breathe on a cold window.
Water in your breath makes the window steam up.
You get water from all drinks and food like fruit.

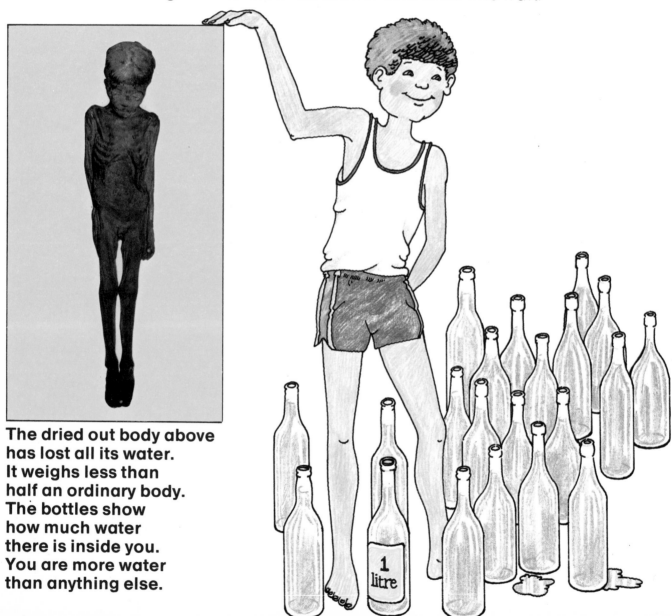

**The dried out body above
has lost all its water.
It weighs less than
half an ordinary body.
The bottles show
how much water
there is inside you.
You are more water
than anything else.**

You use water to wash or if you flush the lavatory,
as well as for drinking and cooking.
The buckets in the picture show how much water
someone uses in this country every day.
Even dry things, like crisps, take lots of water
to make them in a factory.

The water you use comes out of a tap, a river
or a reservoir (a big lake where water is kept
for people to use). The water you drink
should be made clean or it might make you ill.

flushing lavatory and washing yourself

drinking and eating

it takes this much water to make a bag of crisps

4½ litres

CRISPS

Some children carry water home from a well. How much could *you* carry? Would it last all day? If you had to use less, what would you do without? Each bucket holds 4½ litres of water.

When you need to cool down, you sweat more. You sweat a bit most of the time, without noticing it. Even when you sleep, you sweat a little.

A thermometer shows us how hot or cold something is (its temperature). A thermometer is marked in degrees (°C). Find the normal temperature for you.

Your body stays at the same level of warmth, in cold and hot weather. Your body feels hot when you have been running. This is because you make your own heat if you move or work. On a cold day, you need to keep heat in. On a hot day, you need to get rid of heat.

Moving and shivering make more heat, and clothes and warm houses keep the heat in. Sweating cools you down. Do you like to swim in cold water on a hot day? How does it help you? You measure your temperature with a thermometer. If you are ill, your temperature may go up a bit.

If the inside of your body is too hot or cold, it can not work properly. That is why we need to stay at the same temperature.

You and others

We know of a few children who never lived
with other people when they were little.
Nobody cared for them, but they had enough food.
The girl in the photograph is eight years old.
She was found long ago in India. People said she
lived with the wolves.

Later she learnt to stand up, and eat like us.
How would she be different from you?
Some things she would learn by herself.
But *you* learn a lot from other people.
Think of the things she would know nothing about.
The pictures on the right may help you.

Do you ever work in a group of other people
to do a thing you couldn't do alone?
People can often do more if they work together.

**How do these people help
each other?
What else have you learnt
from other people?**

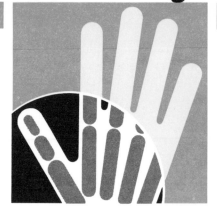

Bones-the hard bits

Your bones are the hard bits of your body.
The rest of you is soft.
You can feel the hardness of bones in your head,
your knee, and the front of your leg.
Your bones are joined together by joints.
Draw round your hand. Mark all the places
where your fingers can bend. These are the joints.
Can you see the joints in the X-ray photograph?

All your bones are joined up to make a skeleton.
Your skeleton holds you up and lets you move.

**How would you look
without your bones?**

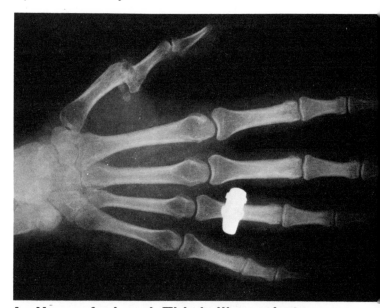

**An X-ray of a hand. This is like a photo
of the bones in the hand. How many bones
are in the hand? Can you see
what is wrong with the thumb?**

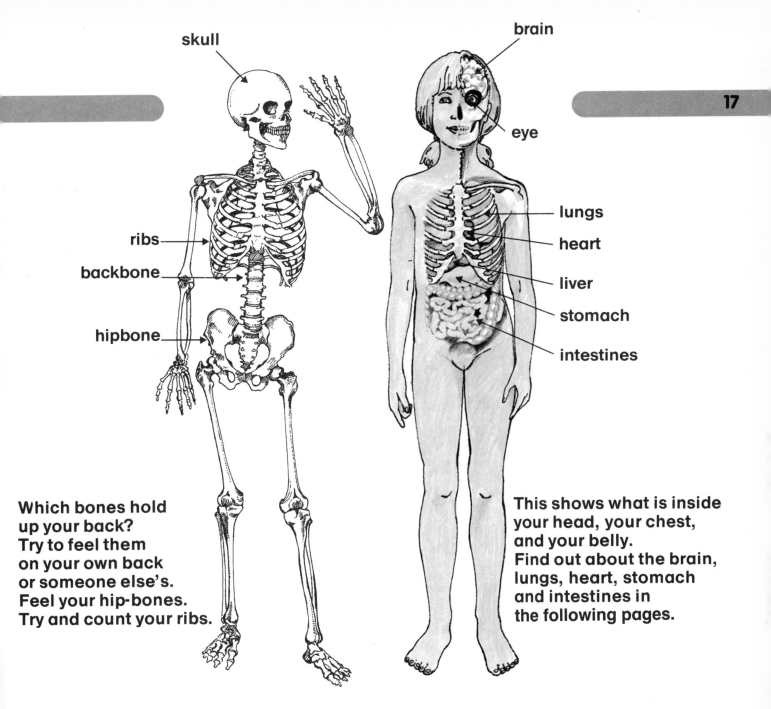

skull

brain

eye

ribs

backbone

hipbone

lungs

heart

liver

stomach

intestines

Which bones hold up your back? Try to feel them on your own back or someone else's. Feel your hip-bones. Try and count your ribs.

This shows what is inside your head, your chest, and your belly. Find out about the brain, lungs, heart, stomach and intestines in the following pages.

As well as holding you up, a skeleton protects your body. Which parts do your ribs and skull protect? Put your hand over your eye. You can feel that the eye is protected by a strong ring of bone with the eyebrow above and the cheekbone below.

Milk helps the hard parts of your bones to grow. This is one reason why all children need milk. Without this food, bones can't grow properly. You get taller as your bones grow longer. Sometimes children mark their height on a wall each year to see how fast they are growing.

What's going on around you?

How do you know about the things around you?
Your senses tell you what is happening around you.
See how Ann in the cartoon is using her senses.

Your brain sorts out what your senses tell you.
It remembers what you have found out before.
Your brain is in charge of everything you do.
You think and decide what to do with your brain.
Another part of your brain tells the heart to pump.
It controls your muscles. Your brain does millions
of other jobs that you don't even notice it doing.

What reminds Ann it is lunchtime and she is hungry?

How does she know she can buy a hamburger?

Ann must cross the road. Which two senses does she use? Do they both say the same things to her?

This boy can not see. How is he reading?

You know what things look like by using your eyes. You see because eyes are sensitive to light: your eye sends signals to your brain about the light. Your brain makes pictures from the signals it gets from your eyes.

You hear music because ears are sensitive to sound: they send signals of the sound to the brain. Where does the brain get smell or taste signals from?

Shut your eyes. What can your skin tell you? The skin on your hands is very sensitive. It can feel cold or hot things or pain. What else?

Ann's hamburger tastes good. What other sense may help her enjoy it?

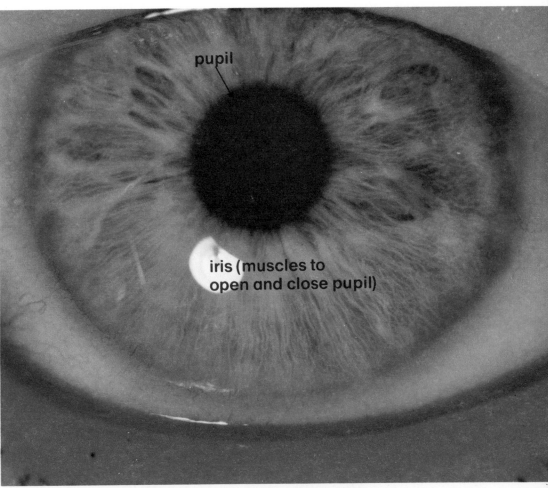

pupil

iris (muscles to open and close pupil)

A pupil lets light into the eye. If it's dark, the pupil opens wide to let in all the light it can. Do you think this eye is looking at bright light?

Muscle power

A body-builder's muscles can be seen more easily than yours. They are built up by special exercises. They are not always as strong as they look.

You move by using muscles fixed onto bones. A muscle works by getting shorter. When it works it feels hard. Put your hand on your cheek in front of your ear. Bite hard with your teeth. You can feel the muscle getting short and hard.

Some muscles work to keep you still. Stand on one leg and move the other. Can you feel the muscles in the leg you are standing on? They are holding your leg straight and steady.

Muscles must work together. Your brain makes them work together by sending orders to each muscle. Some muscles work all the time, even if you sleep. Some are not fixed on to bone, but squeeze tubes inside your body. Your heart, for example, is a muscle that pumps all your blood.

Muscles of different sizes all over your body do different jobs. More than thirty muscles in your face make you frown, smile or squint. The coloured part of your eye is made up of tiny muscles. They control how much much light gets into your eye.

this muscle
pulls lower
part of leg up

this muscle
raises the
heel

this muscle
will straighten
the leg to kick

this
muscle has
straightened
the leg

Lots of different muscles work together
when you make even a simple movement.

As you kick a ball, your brain tells
the muscles what to do. At the same time,
your senses tell the brain how well the leg
is kicking. Your eyes tell the brain how close
the foot will come to the ball. If the brain
decides the foot will miss the ball,
it tells the muscles to adjust the kick.

Breathing

You can make yourself breathe quickly or slowly.
But no one can stop breathing for long. This is
because all the body parts need oxygen all the time.

Air goes into your lungs when you breathe in.
The part of the air you need is called oxygen.
It goes from your lungs into the blood
and is taken all round your body.
Some of the air is no use and you breathe it out.

When you run about, your muscles work hard.
They need more oxygen. How do you get more oxygen?
How does your breathing change when you run about?

When you breathe in, the space inside your chest gets bigger and air rushes in.

You breathe out by making your chest smaller. You can feel this with your hands. Air comes out.

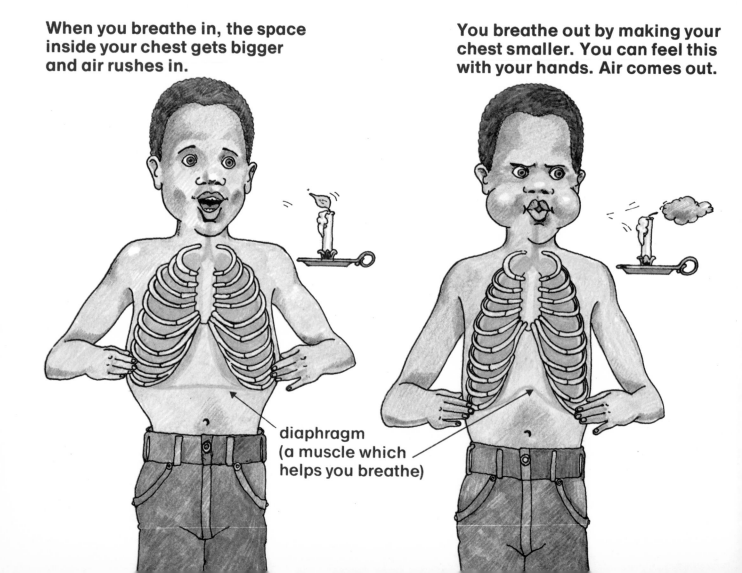

diaphragm
(a muscle which
helps you breathe)

Digesting food

All your body parts need food as well as oxygen. The food you eat is changed before you can use it. This change is digestion and it starts in your mouth.

You mash up food when you chew it. Spit makes it soft and easy to swallow. Your tongue tastes it and when you swallow, your tongue pushes food down your throat. Your gullet takes the food on to the stomach. After staying in the stomach, food is squeezed down a long tube, the intestine.

If your intestine were stretched out straight, it would be four or five times as long as you. It is curled up to fit inside you.

While this happens, the food goes on changing. Now it goes easily through the sides of the tube, into the blood. The blood carries the food to the other parts of the body. Food you can't use goes to the end of the tube. You push it out when you go to the lavatory.

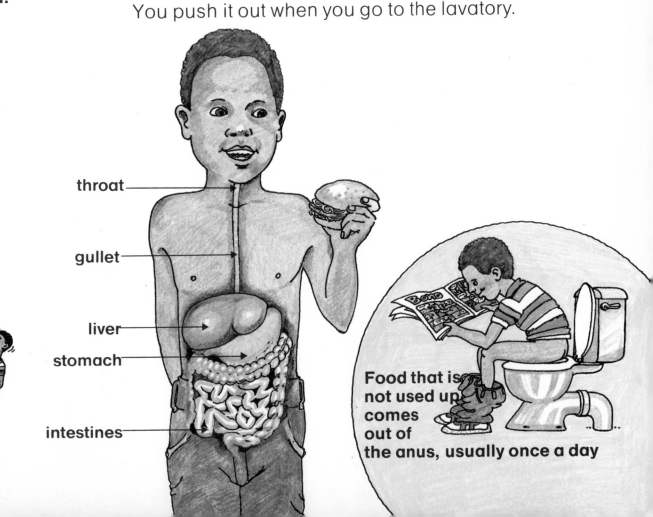

throat

gullet

liver

stomach

intestines

Food that is not used up comes out of the anus, usually once a day

Your heart and blood

Your blood collects oxygen (from your lungs) and food (from your intestines) and delivers them to all the parts of your body that need them. Blood runs in tubes called blood vessels, which are everywhere in your body. When you cut through the skin, you bleed because you have cut into some blood vessels. Your biggest blood vessels are thicker than a crayon.

Blood is pushed along the vessels by your heart, which squeezes or pumps 70-100 times every minute. Blood goes once round your body and then returns to the heart. Then it is pumped to the lungs and on round the body again.

**Your heart looks like this
and is about this size.
Look for the big blood vessels
that take blood in and out of the heart.**

**Stick a drawing pin into a dead match.
Put it on your wrist near your thumb.
Lay your wrist on a table: the match moves
with your pulse as blood pumps along
the blood vessel. You can also feel
your heart beat just under the left nipple.**

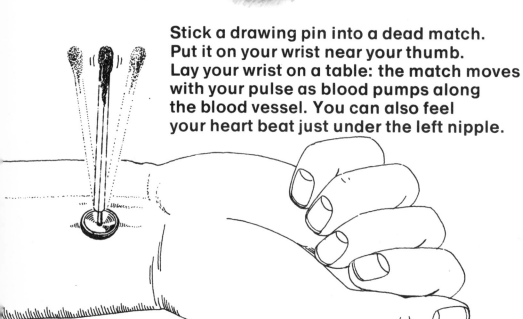

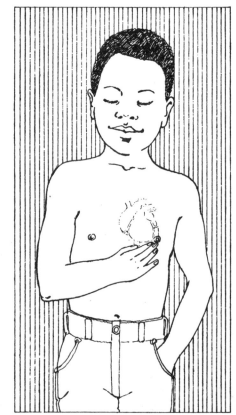

Your blood must keep the right amount of water in it. The kidneys' job is to remove unwanted water if there is too much water in your blood. All your blood goes through your kidneys 20 times an hour.

The kidneys also remove unwanted and dangerous things mixed up in the blood. These go from the kidney down to the bladder, a bag which is held shut by muscles at one end. When it is full of liquid, you go to the lavatory and let it out.

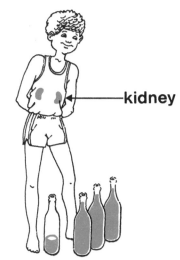

kidney

This is how much blood your body holds. Each bottle holds one litre.

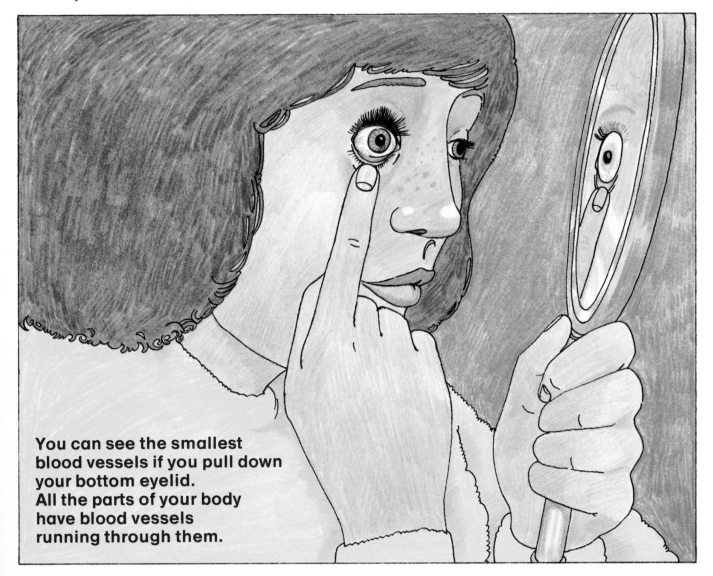

You can see the smallest blood vessels if you pull down your bottom eyelid. All the parts of your body have blood vessels running through them.

Hands, skin and mouths

Look at all the different things these children are using their hands for. How many other things can you do with your hands?

Some parts of your body do many different jobs. Skin covers your body. What else does it do? As well as keeping out dirt and water, your skin keeps your body's water in.

Skin also keeps you cool when it's hot. Lick the back of your hand. Now blow on it. Can you feel it cool your skin?

Prehistoric humans were very hairy. Tiny skin muscles made their hairs stand up to keep warm air close to their skin. This helped keep them warm. We are not so hairy, but our skins still act as if we were hairy. Cold days make the muscles give you tiny skin bumps called goosepimples.

People with pale skins go darker to protect them as long as they are in bright sun. Often the skin does not change quickly enough, and it burns!

A brown person's skin does not often change colour in the sun because it is already protected from the sun. In a country without much sun, a brown person's skin stays brown.

Sometimes the sun is so bright that a person with brown skin goes darker.

What happens to skin in the sun

We all have a chemical in our skins that makes the skin go dark to protect us from dangerous sunlight. Some people have dark skins and others have pale skins. People have dark skins because long ago their grandparents and their grandparents' grandparents lived in very sunny countries. The chemical made their skins go dark to protect them from the sun all the time. Their children had dark skins, because people have the same colour skin as their parents.

People have pale skins because long ago their families lived in countries where the sunlight was not strong, so they did not need dark skin.

**How are these people using their mouths and lips?
How many more things can you do with your mouth? What are you doing with it now?**

Growing up

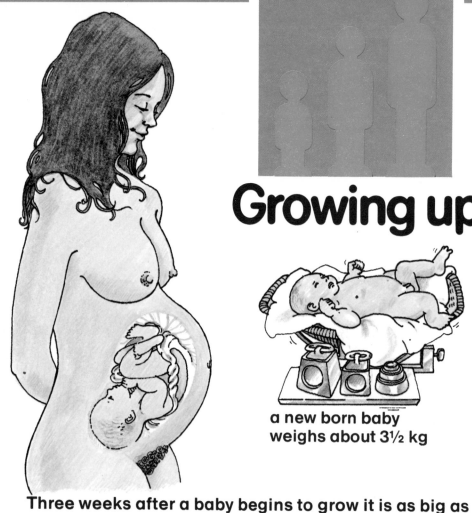

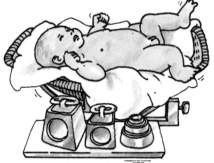

a new born baby
weighs about 3½ kg

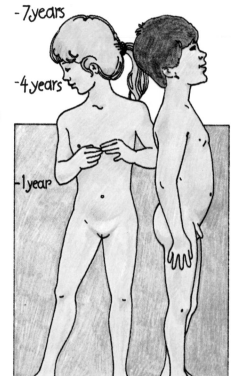

-7 years

-4 years

-1 year

Three weeks after a baby begins to grow it is as big as your finger nail. At birth it will be about 50 cm long.

A baby is born after growing for nine months. It starts growing when sperm from the father joins up with a tiny egg inside the mother. After a baby is born, it still needs a lot of looking after. How many ways can you think of?

Here are a few things you may have learned to do since you were a baby. Put them in the right order, starting with the things you learned to do first.

Running
Riding a bicycle
Kicking a football
Reading

Learning to talk
Walking
Playing with friends
Eating with a spoon

These two seven year old children are about 130 cm tall. How tall are you? Do you know how tall you were one year ago?

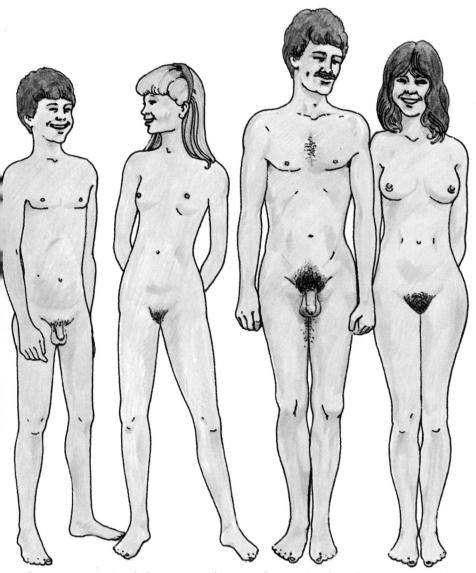

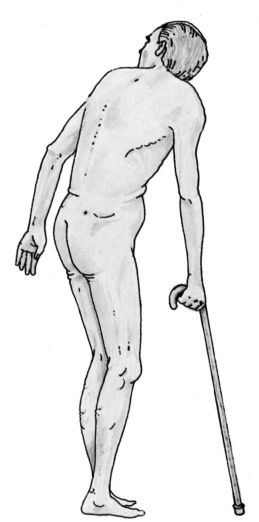

As you get older, you learn how to look after yourself more and more. By the time you leave school, you will want to earn money and lead your own life. You may look for a boyfriend or a girlfriend. Later, you may have children of your own.

At the end of their lives, everyone dies. Their hearts and brains stop working. People who liked and loved them are very sad. Some people believe that a very special part of you goes on living after you die.

As people get old their bodies begin to wear out. Their bones break more easily, joints get stiff and muscles are not so strong.

What is a family? It might be you and your sisters and brothers, uncles, aunts and cousins as well as your mother and father. Or it can be just parents and children living at home.

Look at the photo album below. Families can be a few or many people. What is the biggest family you know?

You see your family at home every day. People in a family can talk to each other and help each other. But you meet lots of other people. How many different people talk to you, work or play with you each day?

Anne and her three brothers live with their mum and dad.

Assim and his baby sister live with their mum and dad.

Peter and Jane live with their mum and dad. Their mum's sister and her children live in the same house and so does grandma.

John lives with his dad.

The people in this family all meet different people during the day. Who do they each meet?
Where do they meet them?

2

Living Together

Anna Sproule

About this chapter

Do you live in a big place with lots of houses, people and shops? Or do you live in a village? Some families live near other people, others live far apart. We all live together in communities.

If you live near other people,
do you help them? How do they help you?
In communities, people do things together.
They share the same schools, hospitals and shops.

When you play games, you follow the rules.
People who live together also need to make rules.
This helps them to get food, shelter and work.

In school, you meet many different children. Learning together helps us understand each other's needs.

Having fun with friends is great. Living together is not all work and no play!

Do you know the people
who live next door to you?
Who live in the same street,
or round the corner?
All these people are
your neighbours.

Some people grow their
own food. They take some
of it to the market
to sell to other people.

What do people need?

A home

If you live in the country, you may live
in a cottage. If you live in a town, you may live
in a house or a block of flats. Not everyone
lives in a house, but nearly everyone has a home.

A home is a place where you can sleep safely,
meet your friends, read a book or play.
If you could choose, where would you like to live?

**These nomads move around to look for food for
their animals. They take their homes with them.**

What jobs need to be done in your home? Who does these jobs? Who helps?

Thousands of years ago, some people lived in caves. Some people in Turkey live in caves today.

A home is where most of your meals are made, and where you meet the other people in your family. What would it be like if you did not have a home?

A home is a place where you can be warm in cold weather, or cool in hot weather.

If you live in a place where it rains a lot, the roof of your home will slope steeply. This will help the rain run off. People need different houses for different places.

Villages and towns

How well do you know your neighbours?
Do you know their names? Do you know what sort
of jobs they do? Are they friendly and helpful?
The place where you all live together
is called a neighbourhood.

A lot of people here know each other just a little,
even if they are not great friends.
Most families go to the same shops.
Most of the children go to the same schools.

In a village, everyone knows everyone else.
A village is just one big neighbourhood. In a town
there are lots of different neighbourhoods.
Neighbours live together in a community.

**This long house in Indonesia is like a small village.
It is the home of many families.**

In a town, there are hundreds of different places where people can earn money, go shopping, meet each other or have fun. In a village, there may be only a few.

Some people would get bored in a village. Others might get lonely in a town, because there are so many people they do not know.

An English village is a small community. What are some of the things going on in the village in this picture?

Hong Kong is a very crowded city. There are many places to buy things. People have many different jobs.

A community

People start living together in a place because there is something there that they want.
For instance, the people who started the community in this picture wanted something that might make them very rich: gold. Later, other people came.

"Gold! Gold! . . . I've found gold!"
This is what happened in Gulgong, Australia in 1870.

"Let's all get there! Quick!"
The great rush begins. Miners hurry to the diggings.

More gold is found. Roads are made. Other people come along too, build shops, sell things and do jobs for the people already there.

Soon there is a bank, lots of houses, a church, more shops, a hotel . . . A community grows . . .

The railway comes too . . . Lots more people come here to stay. The place has become a town.

People and food

We all need to eat and drink. Today,
we buy nearly all the food we eat from shops.
In a big community there are a lot of shops,
so it is always easy to find food you like.
What is it like in a small community?

Even if there are shops in the neighbourhood,
some people grow quite a lot of their own food.

People have to grow or catch their own food
if there are no shops near them at all.
This is more difficult than shopping, and
takes up a lot more time.

Farmers also grow food, mainly to sell to other
people, not to eat themselves.

Today, people still hunt for food, like these fishermen out in the North Sea.

Many thousand years ago, groups of early people followed big animals for food: deer and bisons.

Much later, some people began to keep animals and to settle down.

Harvesting machines in the USA can do the job that many people used to do. Farmers can now grow more food for many more people.

picking and gathering

As well as hunting big animals for food, groups of early people gathered wild plants and berries to eat.

farming

A few thousand years ago, people found out how to grow plants from seeds. There was more food for everybody. Larger groups of people settled down.

People and work

There are hundreds of different jobs people can do.
When they work, they earn money for themselves
and their families.

Everyone who works helps other people to work.
We all help each other do our jobs.
The pictures on these two pages show how many
different workers helped to make Tom's baked beans.
Tom's father, the postman, also has to work
to get money to pay for the beans.

This is the farmer who grows the beans.

People pick tomatoes to make the sauce for the beans.

Steel workers make steel for the can for the beans.

Tree-cutters cut down trees to make paper for the label on the can.

This is the shopkeeper.
He sells baked beans
and lots of other things
as well.

This is Tom.
He is having baked beans for tea.

This is the driver
who takes the beans to the shop.

This is the printer
who prints labels for the can.

This is the canner
who puts the beans in the can.

Where do people live?

A place to live

Would you like to live in the city you can see on this page? What do you think it has to offer? Are there places to work, to learn, to have fun? The pictures underneath show how the city grew over thousands of years.

church

social club

park

offices

In the beginning, people first had to clear the forests to make a home . . .

Thousands of years later, a village had grown. People also began to travel longer distances . . .

The small village has turned into a small town. What new things can you see?

More people have arrived. The town has become a city. It would have looked like this a hundred years ago.

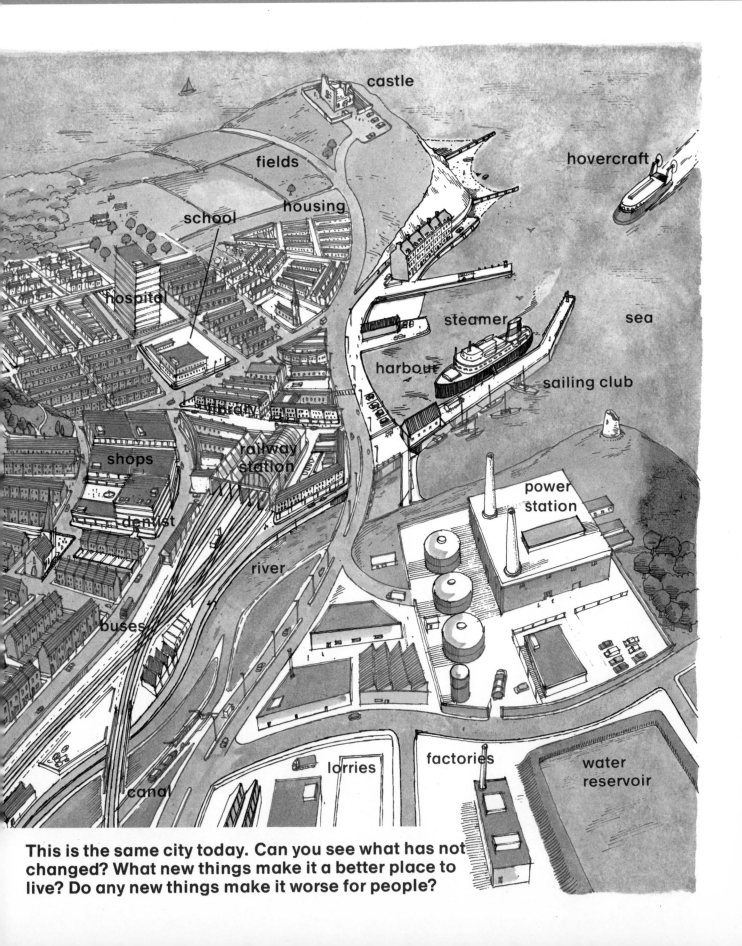

castle

hovercraft

fields

housing

school

sea

hospital

steamer

harbour

sailing club

shops

railway station

power station

dentist

river

buses

lorries

factories

water reservoir

canal

This is the same city today. Can you see what has not changed? What new things make it a better place to live? Do any new things make it worse for people?

On the move

Some people travel long distances to work from one community to another. Others only need to walk across the street. How did you get to school today?

People have always travelled to find food or work. For instance, farmers had to take the things they grew to market towns where they could be sold to other people. They also needed to buy things from shopkeepers there to take back to their farms.

A very full bus in India. People travel between communities for work or to visit their families.

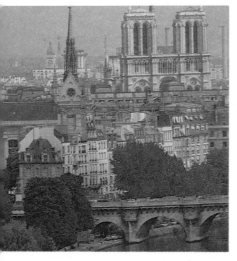

Left. Bridges help to keep people on the move. Many people who live on either side of the river in Paris need to cross the bridge to go to work.

People who had things to sell wanted lots of customers. If they went to places where two roads crossed, they could do business with people coming from different ways. So many people settled down where two roads crossed and communities grew up.

Some people are always on the move. Today, nomads still travel long distances to find food and water for their animals.

People go home by boat after a long day fishing. Travelling is part of the way of life for these people in West Africa. Even their homes are built on the river.

If they all work together, people can often make things better in the place where they live. In some parts of England, they have turned wet, marshy places into dry land. They could grow more food there, and start to build new towns.

But sometimes people make mistakes. Farmers once thought that cutting hedges down meant they would have room to grow even more food. But hedges protect the land. Without them, the earth blows away and farming becomes difficult.

The smoke from the factory nearby drifts into people's homes and makes them bad places to live in.

In the Middle East, people have brought water to the land to enable them to grow crops.

In parts of Ethiopia it is usually very dry. When it gets even drier people and cattle can't live there.

In cities with a lot of factories, there is often plenty of work. But smoke from these factories may make the cities nasty places to live in.

Sometimes, places become difficult to live in even if people do all the right things. If the weather gets worse suddenly, this can change people's lives. If too much rain falls rivers overflow, and floods destroy people's homes and crops.

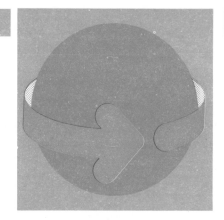

Looking after people

If people are ill, they need looking after.
They also need looking after when they are young,
or when they are very old. Can you count
how many people look after you?

Communities have worked out all sorts of ways
for looking after people. There are schools
for children, and special homes for old people.
There are also homes for people who are disabled
and cannot do things for themselves.

When a child is born, the health visitor calls on mother and child to give advice and check that both are healthy.

This doctor has to travel around visiting lots of families in Africa.

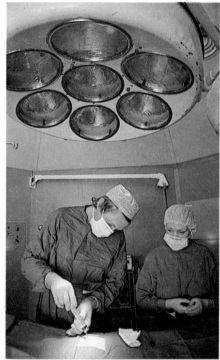

It costs a lot of money to have hospitals like this one. Good doctors and nurses all help to make it work well.

This teenager is helping an old man in his home. Old people are often lonely. They may like visits from friends and neighbours.

You know what happens if you fall and break your leg! In hospitals, doctors and nurses are all specially trained to look after people.

But families and neighbours all help too.
Can you think how?
Do you help to look after anyone living near you?

Keeping warm...or cool

On a really cold day, what do people do to keep warm?
They close the windows of their house to keep
the cold out. They light a fire or turn up the heating
to keep their homes warm.

Houses in very hot countries often have small
windows. It's the sun that people want to keep out
here, not the cold. But if there is a cool wind,
people might leave the windows open.
Then the wind can blow right through and make them
feel cooler.

**This clay house in Iran has no windows.
Summers are hot in Iran. The walls
keep the sun out so it stays cool
inside the house.**

**In countries with lots of forests
and very cold winters, many
of the houses are built from wood.
This keeps the heat in very well.**

Eating and drinking

A Chinese family having a meal. Some of the food they are eating may be different from what you are used to eating.

Tomorrow, count how many different things you eat in a day. If you can, find out which country they came from to begin with.

Today, many of us eat food that comes from all over the world. We buy it in shops. But a long while ago, most people ate food grown nearby.

People in different countries ate the food they could grow best. If they did not grow it themselves, they usually bought it at a market.

Making rules

In your house, who decides what everyone eats every day? Perhaps you do – sometimes. How would you feel in your playground if one person always wanted to make all the rules? And what would you do if you did not agree with them?

Decisions have to be made in the community too. Often, just a few people make the decisions. But a community is a much better place to live in if everyone can say what they think the decisions should be.

Who decides?

at home

at school

in the community

at work

in the country

In all homes, in schools and towns, people have to decide what to do, and when it is to be done. Communities choose people to make rules for them.

Children in London are asking the people who make the rules for the schools they need.

Having fun

All people need to do things they like.
Sometimes, they like having fun in a crowd:
they play games, or go to parties, or just sit
around and talk. Sometimes, they prefer doing
something on their own: they go for a walk,
watch television or read a book.
People also like going out: to a football match,
camping, swimming, or having fun in the park.

**Big cities have lots of places where people can enjoy themselves.
That's often why people like living there.**

3

Different Peoples

Anna Sproule

About this chapter

This chapter is about you. It is also about many other
people. People who live in different places do
some things differently from the way you do them.
And they do some things in just the same way.
This book will tell you about some customs,
beliefs and ways of life that groups of people
have in some parts of the world. We call customs,
beliefs and ways of life our culture.

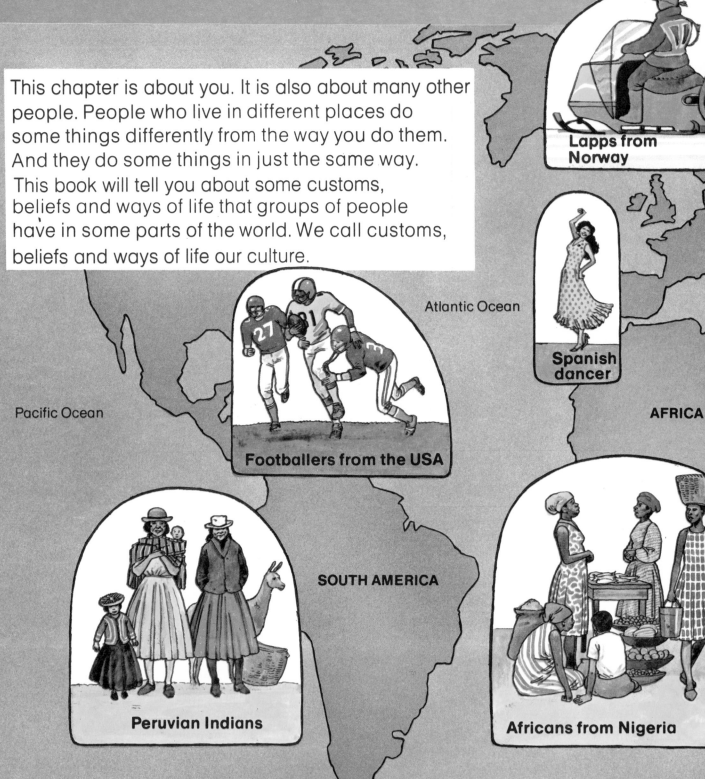

Lapps from Norway

Spanish dancer

Atlantic Ocean

AFRICA

Pacific Ocean

Footballers from the USA

SOUTH AMERICA

Peruvian Indians

Africans from Nigeria

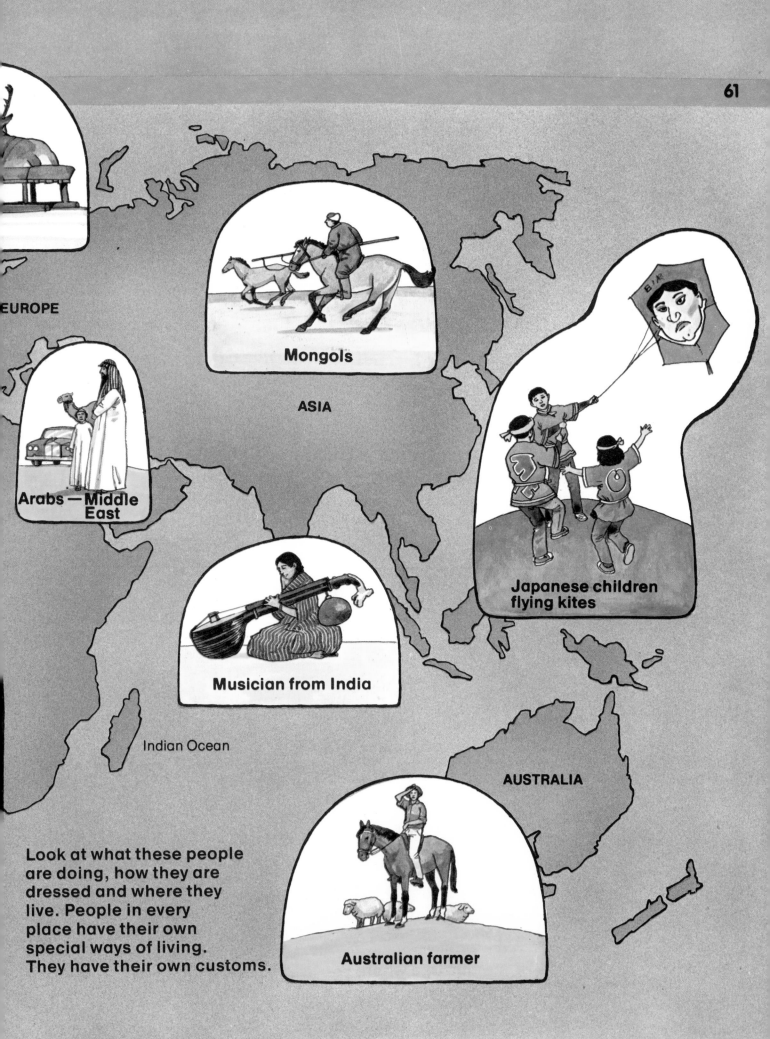

EUROPE

Mongols

ASIA

Arabs — Middle East

Musician from India

Japanese children flying kites

Indian Ocean

AUSTRALIA

Look at what these people are doing, how they are dressed and where they live. People in every place have their own special ways of living. They have their own customs.

Australian farmer

How do you live?

People who live in different places often wear different clothes for special occasions.
What clothes do you wear at school?
In some schools, children wear a uniform.
In other schools, they don't.

The sort of clothes we wear and the sort of food we eat are all part of our culture.

Skipping is a game usually played by girls rather than boys. Is this true where you live?

In France, shops sell bread in many shapes
but many loaves are long and thin.
In Britain, they are usually shorter and fatter.
In India, many people eat a sort of pancake instead.
They call it a chappati.

Do you have any friends from other countries?
If you do, ask them what they ate at home yesterday.

People have different holidays too.
In Scotland, and a lot of other places, the
beginning of theNew Year is an important holiday.
Does your family do anything special
on New Year's Eve? Do they let you join in?

Christians celebrate the birth of Jesus Christ at Christmas.

In Scotland, men often wear a kilt. It looks like a skirt. In lots of countries, women wear trousers.

The festival of Diwali is a holiday for Indian children. Lights are lit to decorate houses. People have parties and let off fireworks.

Customs

The way people do special things on special occasions is called a custom. For a birthday, for instance, they may dress up, make cakes and invite friends.

A birthday party would not be the same without a birthday cake and its candles: one for every year. Having the cake and lighting the candles is a custom. It is something that many people in Britain and other places always do on their children's birthdays.

A birthday party is a popular custom in many countries.

Customs are an important part of a people's
culture. They are not only about food.
Kite flying, for instance, is a popular custom in Japan
Customs can be about clothes, holidays and work.

Sometimes customs are about all these things
together. Christmas is a holiday – and at
a Christmas party people pull crackers, wear
paper hats and ask each other riddles. A lot
of people have Christmas parties at work, too.

**It is the custom for
Chinese people to eat
special cakes during
the Moon festival.**

**Americans have a special
holiday in November called
Thanksgiving Day. For
dinner, they have turkey
and pumpkin pie.**

How we feel

Would you play a game you liked even if your friends laughed at you? Thinking some games are silly is an attitude. Thinking some games are not right for boys or girls is another one. Many people think a game like skipping is only for girls. Attitudes are an important part of our culture

All over the world, people have different ideas about what looks nice, or about what is polite, or about what is the right thing to wear. An attitude is what you feel about something. Thinking that the things some people do are strange is an attitude too.

In India, the polite way to greet people is to join hands.

German business people shake hands a lot!

Hugging is one way of greeting friends in Russia.

Bowing is a traditional way of greeting people in Japan.

Attitudes change, just as customs do. People in some communities think it is wrong for women to go out to work at a job. They think women should stay at home and look after the house and children. But a great many women have jobs now.

Young people may have different attitudes about things from those of their parents. They may have their own views about how to behave, what to wear, what food they like, what books to read and about how to choose friends.

People used to think that cooking was a woman's job. But many boys are taught to cook today.

Do you like the hair-styles in these pictures? What do your parents think about them?

What we believe

People have always asked questions about why
we are alive and what happens after death.
Different religions have given different answers.
But, whatever their beliefs, many religious people
gather around a leader in a special place of worship.

Religions are about beliefs in a god or in
many gods. Christians, Jews and Muslims
believe in one God. Hindus worship one God who
appears to people in different ways. Buddhists,
like the others, follow sets of rules which
shape their way of life.

**Between the ages of eight and eleven, some
Hindu boys receive a sacred thread.
The priest hangs it round their body.
This means that they are ready to learn
more about their religion.**

**Confirmation allows these
Christians to take full
part in the rites of
their religion.**

The Ka'aba is a shrine in Mecca. Muslims try to go to the city of Mecca to pray at the Ka'aba once during their life. Muslims call God Allah.

Most religious people take part in ceremonies like weddings and funerals.
In many religions, people are asked to be kind and helpful to others.

Religion is very important to many people. Some people's faith is so strong that they have fought and died for their beliefs.

Superstitions

If you spill some salt, do you throw it over your shoulder? Lots of people believe that spilling salt is unlucky. But, if you throw some salt over your shoulder, the bad luck will go away.

This is a British superstition. A superstition is partly a custom, partly a belief. All cultures have some.

Chinese artists drew dragons to represent everything good and strong. But for Christian artists, dragons used to stand for sin.

Some Americans take great care when they are out not to walk on cracks in the pavement. American children have a rhyme about this: "Step on a crack—Break your mother's back."

The Ancient Egyptians thought that cats were holy. But later, the first Christians thought that anything to do with old religions was bad. So cats were then often thought of as unlucky.

Points up, a horseshoe is lucky; points down, it's unlucky.

A black cat is unlucky in America, but lucky in Britain.

In Spain, eating twelve grapes on New Year's Eve brings luck for a year.

In Italy, some flowers are used only for graves.

How cultures grow

Tales that travel

Do you know how this rhyme started?
"Ring-a-ring-of roses, a pocketful of posies,
Atishoo! Atishoo! We all fall down!"
The rhyme described what happened over 300 years ago
to people who died of a terrible illness called
the plague. They got a rose-pink rash on their
skins. They sneezed, and then fell down. People
thought that sniffing a bunch of flowers would
keep the plague away. That was what the "posies" were for.

"Oranges and lemons,' say the bells of
St Clement's. You owe me five farthings,
say the bells of St Martin's."
The rhyme of this game has been passed
on to children for 200 years.

Children learn a lot about their family's history from their grandparents.

So the words of the rhyme mean something that a lot of people have forgotten. They used to be about something frightening, but now they are just a playground game.

A lot of customs and beliefs start as one thing and end up as something else.
The same thing happens with stories. They change as they get passed on from one group of people to another.

True or made-up tales about King Arthur and his Knights can still be read today.

Tradition and change

In many places where Christmas is a holiday, people put up Christmas trees. The custom of bringing evergreens into the house began many hundreds of years ago to celebrate mid-winter.

The Christmas tree is not always covered in snow as it is on Christmas cards. In Australia, for example, it is hot at Christmas. These pictures show how we think the custom grew and changed.

The Romans decorated their houses with twigs of evergreens during the winter celebrations.

The first Christmas trees with candles were seen in the homes of German families after 1700.

Queen Victoria's husband, Prince Albert, started the custom of Christmas trees at Windsor Castle in the 1840s.

Christmas in Australia is usually celebrated outdoors, in the sun, but the Christmas tree is still there today.

Why are people different?

Why do we do some things in the same way as other people, and why do we do some things differently? The main reason has to do with the way customs and attitudes begin.

People everywhere have the same needs for food, water and clothes. They need friends, and a home. They need to have fun, play music and dance. But they do all these things in their own way.

The Peruvian Indians shown on the map are farmers just like the Australian man. But the climate and land of their two countries are very different.

In this part of China, people grow a lot of rice, so it is their most important food. In Europe, bread is usually the most important food.

grubs

sheep's eyes

snails

haggis

Does the thought of eating any of these foods make you feel awful? It all depends on where you come from and what you are used to.

The Peruvians grow crops in a very rocky land. They also keep llamas to carry heavy things, and to provide them with meat and wool. Australians have lots of grass for their large flocks of sheep.

Both peoples breed animals for food and wool but the Peruvians only provide food for themselves. Australians produce more than enough to sell to other countries.

People live in a way that fits in best with the place where they live. They develop different cultures which are suited to their own way of life.

Many people are frightened by death. The Ancient Egyptians prepared for it by decorating their tombs and choosing the things they would need in the next world.

Leaders and followers

Do you have friends who can always tell you
what to do? And do you do what these friends tell you?
People like that are leaders. They may sound bossy,
but they are also important.

When you teach a game to someone who doesn't
know it, you are handing on part of your culture.
When your parents tell you to be polite, they
are handing on part of their culture to you. We all
help to share our culture with each other.

**The clothes and hairstyles of the Beatles were
copied by millions of fans in the 1960s.**

**The priest tells people
how they should think
about God. People go to
church to pray.**

This African chief was chosen by his people to make rules for the community. He helps to keep alive the customs and traditions of his people.

People may have different attitudes on how to behave, on what to wear, what to eat or how to have fun. Leaders are persons whose own way of thinking or doing things is followed by a lot of people.

The pictures show you some examples of different leaders: the pop group, the priest and an African chief. In their own ways, they all help to change or keep a group's culture.

Ceremonies

At weddings in Lapland, the bride and groom wear colourful traditional clothes.

All people everywhere have a few very special moments in their lives. Your birthday is one example. Do you invite friends on your birthday and have a party?

In almost every culture in the world, people celebrate at least some of these special moments: they may give presents, or have a party. Sometimes, there is a religious service as well. These celebrations are often called ceremonies.

In some places in Africa, children have to go through special ceremonies before people will accept them as young grown-ups. Some Christian children take part in a religious growing-up ceremony, confirmation.

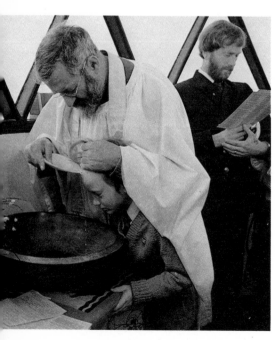

The child is being baptized. He is now accepted as a Christian.

This Jewish boy is preparing for his Barmitzvah. During the ceremony he will read aloud the beliefs of his religion.

Japanese children wear their best clothes for the ceremony of "seven-five-three". This is when parents thank the spirits for keeping their children healthy.

Weddings are usually occasions for a special ceremony and a family gathering. In India, a Hindu bride wears a red sari, and puts a red spot on her forehead. She and her husband give each other garlands. After the wedding, everyone is invited for a large meal and a lot of music is played.

During a Hindu wedding, the priest and the couple sit round a sacred fire. The priest sings prayers. A knot is tied between the bride and groom's clothes and they walk around the sacred fire.

Teaching and learning

You do a lot of things every day. You eat, play,
go to school, talk to people. You may not know it,
but you are learning all the time.
In school, you learn how to read and write.
When you play a game, you are learning the game's
rules. When you eat, you are learning several
things: how to behave at table, and how food
should be prepared.

All these things are part of your culture.
As you grow up, you start teaching some of them
to other people.

**This teacher is showing an English
boy how to play an African drum.**

**This boy from New Guinea is playing
a game. At the same time he is
learning how to throw spears.**

Learning to write in Japan.

4

Fun and Games

Belinda Hollyer

About this chapter

Why do people play games? Almost everyone likes to play. You probably have a favourite way to enjoy yourself. Perhaps this depends on where you live, or what you have to play with, or who you can to play with. Do you play the same games with adults as your friends?

The people in this picture are having fun in different ways. Some are playing with friends, others are playing alone. People are playing games together in teams, listening to music, and reading. What do you like best?

Come and play!

Time for fun

Not everyone has the same amount of time for fun.
Some people have almost no time at all, they have
so much work to do. Who do you play with at school?
Do you play with the same people at weekends?

People who have lots of time can choose what to do.
Some things people do for fun may seem strange
to you. Would you like to struggle up steep rocks
in snow, rain and slashing winds? Mountaineers do.
The harder the climb, the better they like it!

**Childen often play with
whatever is lying around.
An old tyre makes a hoop
for this boy to bowl.**

What do you do in the evening?

Holidays are a good time for fun and games.
Some people go off with their families on holiday.
Does all your family have a holiday together?
What do your parents like to do on holiday?
Are they the same things you like to do?

Some holidays are shared by everyone in a town
or a country. Families, friends and neighbours take
time off work to join in the parades and games.
In Spain every town has a special day once a year,
when people dress up in unusual costumes, or
dance to the music of bands, or just have fun!

**We spent a holiday in Italy.
On Monday we had a picnic
near some lovely old towers
in the country**

**The next day we visited a town and watched
a special flag-throwing festival.**

Play with us!

Many people like competing against each other. Sometimes just two or three are enough for a game, but team games often need lots of people.

You have to learn to play team games. Some games are easy to learn, others take years. You could start learning them now, but you would be grown up before you could play them really well.

Not all these games are played outside. Games like chess or ludo need only small boards and counters. Which board games do you like best? Do you still enjoy the board games you played when you were younger, or do you prefer harder games?

Even a simple game like piggy-in-the-middle needs skills. You have to jump and catch well to be good at this game.

Few Japanese houses have bathrooms. Once or twice a day, people wash together in public baths. It's also a chance for a chat and a game of go-bang.

Buzkashi is a very popular sport
in Afghanistan. Two teams struggle to carry
off a dead calf's body and put it in goal.
Many people in Afghanistan ride horses,
because there are few cars or roads.
Buzkashi is rough and fierce,
but it is a very skilful game.

Come and watch!

It can be fun to watch other people work or play.
Do you ever watch people working in the street?

Games can become work for some of the people
who play them. If you are very good at playing
a game, you might be able to earn a living
doing it. You will have to start when you are young,
and practise very hard. All the separate
parts of the game are very important. You need
to be good at them all.

If others enjoy watching you, they may pay
to see you play. Thousands more may watch you
play on television. Games watched by many people
are often called spectator sports.
Are you a player or a spectator?

**Perhaps we enjoy watching
people work because we
don't have to do it
ourselves! It's much easier
watching than doing.**

At first, she just has fun with a racquet and ball.

At school her teacher helps her to learn the game and shots.

Later on her game gets better and she wins a school competition.

Now she plays all over the world. People pay to come and watch her.

These pictures show how one person might become a famous tennis star. As well as talent, lots of hard work is needed. She must practise hard for years.

Playing to work

Many games teach you skills. Games like chess
help you to think and plan ahead. To start, you learn
the parts of the game, or how each piece moves.
But there's more to it than that! When you make
a move, you must try to guess your partner's next move.
If you're good, you can lay traps for your partner.

Games often teach you how to do things
you will need when you grow up. Do you play
games with words? Many adults enjoy
word games as well, such as crossword puzzles.

**Because she thinks ahead, this girl
realises she could lose
her game of chess
through her first move.**

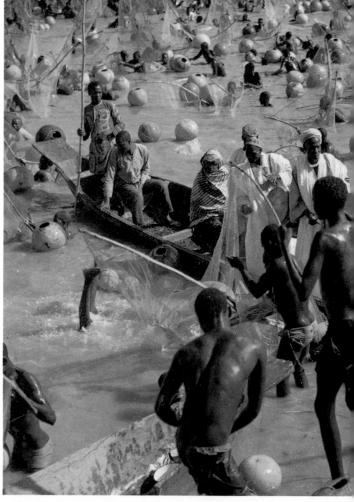

**Fishing is hard work, but some men
in Nigeria start the fishing season
with a festival. There is a prize
for the biggest fish caught.**

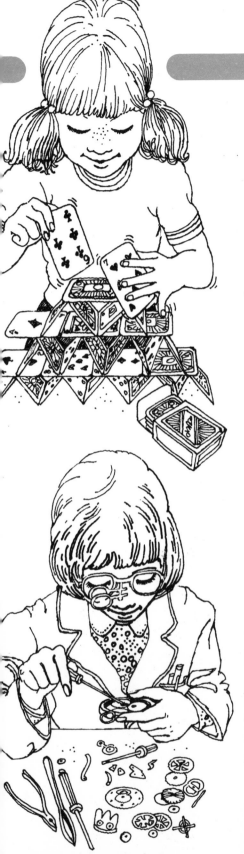

Are you skilful at one sort of game or hobby?
It might be useful when you grow up. Stamp-dealers
often begin by collecting stamps as a hobby.
Many zoo workers kept pets when they were young.

Adults play games when they are training to do
difficult or dangerous work. They must know how
to do the job properly, without making mistakes.
A game like this teaches people before they start
the real work. They can practise everything
until they get it exactly right every time.

**If you enjoy games
that need delicate hands,
it may help you
when you get a job.
If you like to play
outside, you may like
to work outside.**

**If an oil tanker sinks, it's a very expensive mistake!
Some captains learn to sail tankers on models.**

Playing together

Do you make up games to play with your friends?
Lots of people get ideas for games from stories
or films. They use the ideas to start with,
and make up the rest as they go along.
Who decides what everyone does in your game?
Do you take turns, or is it usually the same person
who leads and who makes up the rules?

Some games have winners and losers. If you play
team games, everyone has to agree on the rules.

Why do we have teams? Some people are good
at one thing, others are better at different things.
Everybody puts their special skills together.
A team becomes a bit like a machine, with lots
of separate parts doing different things,
but all working together.

If you play 'cowboys and indians', you don't need any equipment, just friends and imagination!

Knucklebones, jacks, fives – no matter what you call it, children play it everywhere to see who's the best.

Building a tree house needs many skills. Everyone must plan and work together. It helps if someone makes sure that everyone sticks to the plan!

What shall we play?

Learning a game

Look at the children on the cover of this book.
Hopscotch is good to play in towns. You can use
the paving stones in streets for the squares.
Hopscotch takes many different skills. You need
to throw a stone, and balance on one foot.
Then you must jump, turn and bend on one foot.
At first, each bit is hard. But after a while
you can do them all without thinking.

How a New Zealand stick game works

**Knock your sticks against
your partner's sticks.**

**Start the game by putting
your sticks flat on the
ground. Then tap the ends
on the ground in time
with your partner.**

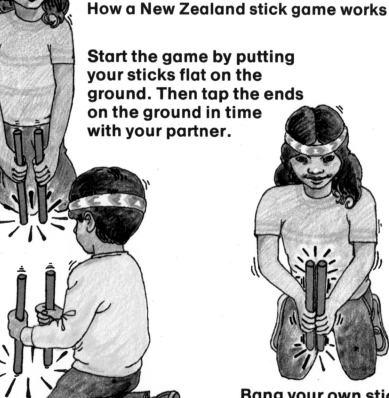

**Bang your own sticks
together in time
with your partner.**

In many games it seems hard to put all
the bits together. Have you ever learned a dance?
Can you remember all the steps for it? You
probably did them slowly to start with.
Then you learnt to do them in time to the music.
Look at the pictures of a New Zealand stick game.
It may look baffling to watch expert players
flip and throw their sticks in time to the music.
But try it bit by bit, and it's not really so hard!

Now put the whole game together. A friend could clap in time for you. Try two taps with your sticks, throw and catch one and start again. Then flip and tap three times on the ground. Make up your own patterns.

Throw one stick to your partner and catch the stick your partner throws back to you. If you're really good, try throwing both sticks at once and catching both your partner's sticks.

Games and rules

Do you argue if someone cheats? Maybe the cheat thought you cheated! That's why games often need rules. But even if you have rules, you must be sure everyone agrees on them before you start. Friends may know different rules for the same game.

If you make up a game you can work out the rules as you go along. The first rules that you thought up can be changed if they are too easy or too hard.

Backgammon is played by nearly everyone in Middle Eastern countries like Egypt. Rich people in Europe sometimes play the game for lots of money in expensive clubs.

If you play toy soldiers you don't really need any proper rules.

Some games are played all over the world. We think chess began in India over a thousand years ago. When people moved around, they took good games with them. As chess spread across the world, some of the rules changed. Now there are different versions of chess, such as Japanese chess and Chinese chess, with different rules. Draughts is a bit like chess, but simpler. It uses a chess board, but the counters are the same as the counters used in backgammon.

Adults play war games with hundreds of rules. This man will replay a real battle to see who would have won if, say, the weather had been different on the day of the battle.

Making your own fun

People have always invented games for themselves. You don't need complicated rules or special equipment. You can use things around you. Do you like to dress up in mum's or dad's old clothes?

Have you ever enjoyed yourself playing follow-my-leader? Children all over the world play this and the 'followers' must do exactly what the leader does. Eskimos play a game where the 'followers' must put their feet in the leader's footprints in the snow. You can be, or do, anything you like with these sort of games. Before people had televisions or radios, they often made their own fun. In the long winter evenings, people used to tell stories to the whole family. Sometimes people used games to tell stories. Ask an old person what sort of things people did before they had television sets.

Cat's cradle is played in countries all over the world. This Eskimo is using string patterns to tell his story. Exactly the same patterns are used for other stories by different people in Africa, America and islands in the Pacific Ocean.

You can build castles in your mind – but it's fun to try out your ideas in sand on a beach.

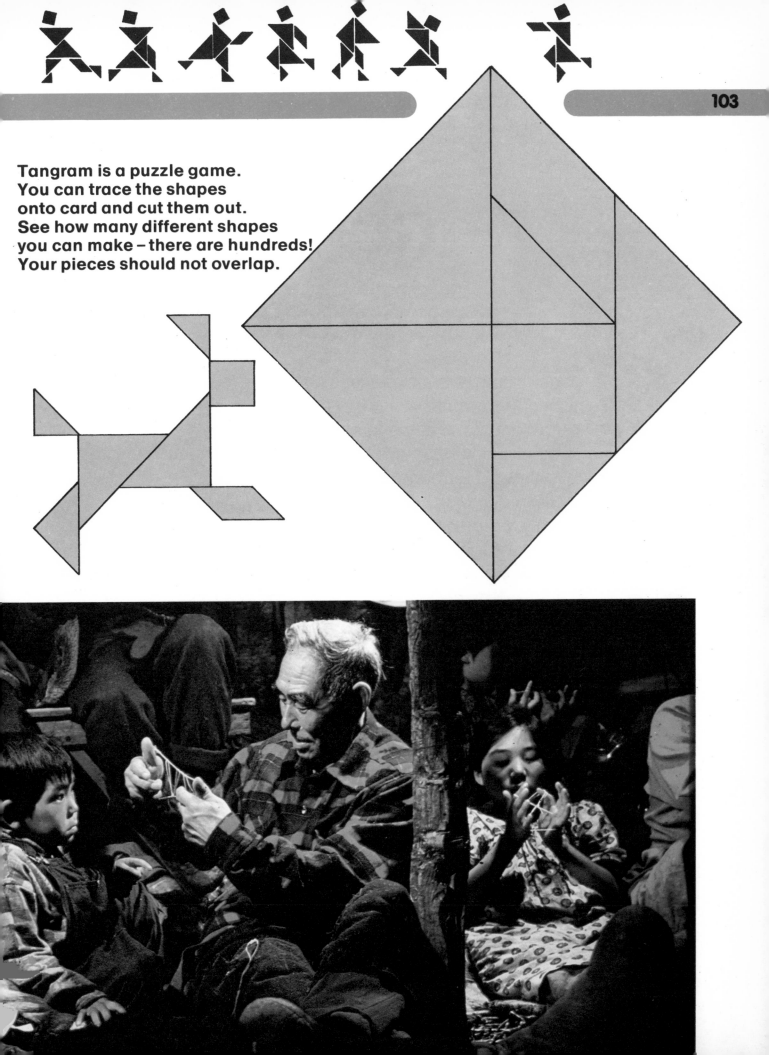

Tangram is a puzzle game.
You can trace the shapes
onto card and cut them out.
See how many different shapes
you can make – there are hundreds!
Your pieces should not overlap.

Games for everyone

It sounds fun

Musical fun is best when it's shared
with other people. Almost everyone in the world
enjoys music of some kind. You need music
to sing and dance, and these are hundred
of different instruments to play.

**You can turn yourself into a band if you really try –
but it's easier, and more fun, playing with others!**

Have you ever been to a concert? People like listening to music as well as making their own. There are bands, orchestras or singers to choose from. What do you like best? Is it music you hear everyday with your friends? Do you like music you enjoyed as a baby? As people get older, the sort of music they like often changes.

You may think another country's music is all groans and squeaks. People from that country may think your music is all thumping and shouting!

Would you like to play in a band? It's not impossible – this band's drummer is only thirteen.

Bamboo grows in Indonesia, where this orchestra comes from. The instruments may seem unusual, but to these children, a piano may seem strange.

It looks fun

Do you watch plays or puppets on television?
It's often more fun to watch real live actors
or puppets. Some old plays, like Punch and Judy,
have been acted the same way for centuries.
Everybody knows what happens next – half the fun
is joining in to tell the actors what comes next.
You can't do that with television!

**Over 300 years ago real actors played Punch
and Judy in Italy. Actors travelled to France
and England, and on the way changed it
into a puppet play.**

20p each in
the HAT for
— Mr PUNCH —

PRIZES for
the LUCKY TICKETS

NEXT SHOW
12·30

Do you like acting stories with your friends?
Do you like to make people laugh, or make them sad,
or even scare them? Usually an audience does not
know what will happen when it sees a play. Actors
all over the world enjoy themselves pretending
to be other people, and trying to get an audience to
share in their game of make-believe.

Some plays are very serious. They have special
meanings that remind people about their beliefs
or history. Have you ever seen a nativity play?
It reminds people that Christmas celebrates
the birth of Jesus, two thousand years ago.

**Wear a home-made mask
and practise your evil
movements in front of
a mirror, and you'll
soon be ready to scare
your friends
as the wicked magician!**

**Has a clown ever scared you? Did you laugh
in relief when you realised it was just a joke?**

Parties and celebrations

Have you ever been to a birthday party,
or had one of your own? A birthday marks the day
when someone was born. Some parties are held
to celebrate a god, others mark the start or end
of a season of the year. We call these festivals.
Many countries have festivals when everyone has a
holiday, and celebrates in the streets or at home.

People celebrate in hundreds of different ways.
They may have parades with banners and flags,
and wear special costumes. They may eat special
food which they only eat at this time.
Sometimes dances, music and plays are kept just
for celebrations. But one thing is the same
everywhere – parties and festivals are shared
with other people. When people celebrate anything,
they like to do it together.

Trinidad's carnival marks the end of winter. Chinese people all over the world have special New Year parades. The two festivals are shown together in this picture. The dragon belongs to the Chinese New Year, and the children in front are dressed up for their own parade through the streets of Trinidad.

Holi festival happens at the start of India's hot season. It celebrates part of the life of a god called Krishna. Everybody gets soaked and covered in coloured powders. By the end of the day they all need a bath!

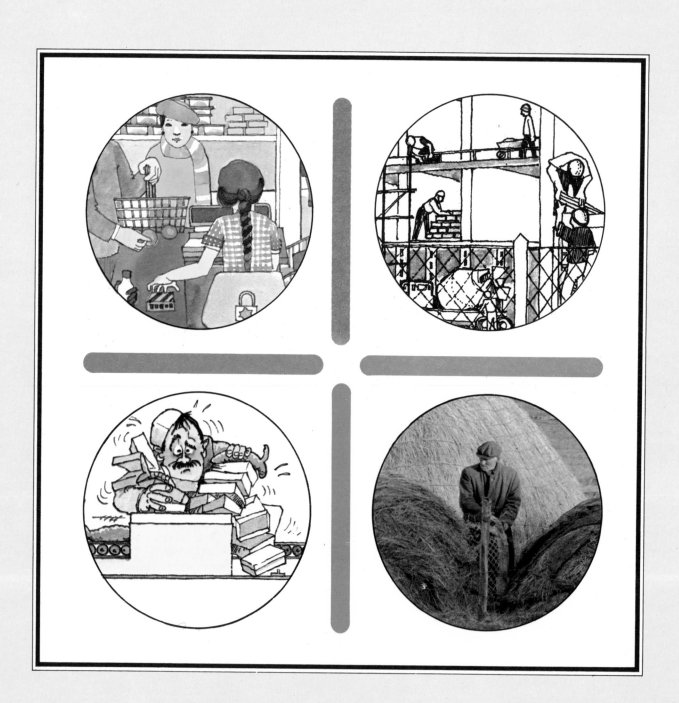

Work

Alistair Ross

About this chapter

Do you work? What kind of work do you do?
Perhaps you work at school and help at home.
Farmers, shopkeepers and drivers are a few
of the workers we know. What other work
is done by people you know?

Why do people work? Most people work for money.
Some people earn much more money than others.
Some don't get paid at all. Many people enjoy
their work and they like meeting the people
they work with. Most people have more than
one reason for working.

**It isn't only children who work in school.
Teaching can be hard work too.
Who else works in a school?**

Some people spend most of their time working at home. Others go out to work.
People often work together to get jobs done. It can be more friendly and often more is done. Other people work on their own.

Older people can give up work. This is called retiring. Some people, such as artists and writers may spend all their lives at work. People such as footballers and pilots can only work really well when they are young. They usually retire early but they may find another job where they don't need to be so fit.
This chapter is about the different ways that people work and how they work together.

All these people want jobs. Not everyone can find a job. We say they are unemployed.

When do people work? Most of us work in the daytime, but there are people who do their jobs at night.

Work at home

There is a lot of work to be done at home. In some families, one person does all this work on their own. There is more cooking, shopping and cleaning for a big family than a small one. It is easier if the work is shared. Which jobs can you do at home? Which jobs are too difficult or dangerous for you to do alone?

In some countries, it is mostly the women who do the housework. The men go out to earn money for the things the family needs. Sometimes it is the other way round. But very often, both men and women go out to work.

This woman is using a washing dolly.
Before washing machines were invented it took hours
of hard work to clean clothes by hand.

There is some cleaning,
cooking and washing-up
to do every day. Other
jobs like decorating
are not done so often.

Housework is only paid for if it is done in someone
else's home. These servants each had special jobs to do.

Workers we know

Wherever you go, you find people working.
Here are six workers. Do you know anyone who
does these jobs? We all need people like these.

Drivers move goods or people from place to place.
They may drive people to work in buses or trains.
They may take goods around the country or abroad.
This man drives a lorry.
Shop assistants sell many of the things we need.
This shop assistant sells all kinds of groceries.
A factory worker might help make anything from
a motor bike ... to a doughnut. This woman works
in a factory where she packs boxes.

driver

shop assistant

factory worker

**There have been shopkeepers for hundreds of years.
This is what one butcher's shop looked like
over a hundred years ago.**

farmer

policewoman

entertainer

Farmers grow plants and rear animals that we need for food and clothing. This farmer works on a dairy farm in England.

The police help us in many ways. They try to arrest people who may have broken the law. They help us if we are burgled or when there is an accident. This policewoman works in a busy city.

Entertainers work to give us pleasure. This woman has a television programme every week in which she sings, dances and tells jokes.

The Bahamas

Brazil

Hong Kong

Fiji

Every country in the world has a police force. They may look different in their uniforms but they all do the same work.

Things we need

Do-it-yourself

What do we need in order to live? We all need
food, drink, clothes and somewhere to live.
We also want fuel or energy to keep us warm,
to cook our food and to work machines like trains
and televisions.

There are some families in the world who
only have what they can make for themselves.
They grow their own food, build their own homes
and make their own clothes and cooking pots.
Very few people live like this today.

**This man has a small farm in Ireland. He works hard
all year round to make many of the things he needs.**

People began to find it easier to do a few jobs well. They could swap what they produced, with other people who had things they wanted. Money helped to make these exchanges fair. There are still many countries where people make most of what they need. They buy only a few things from other people, like cloth and tools.

Can you imagine trying to make all the things you need for yourself? It is very hard work.

On the farm

There are farmers in every country. They may grow crops for us to eat like rice and apples, or they may grow crops that can be turned into cloth, like cotton. Some farmers look after animals that we need for milk and meat. The hide and wool can also be used to make clothes.

The type of farming that is done depends on where the farmer lives and what the people like to eat. Many crops will grow only in places where the weather and soil are just right.

Dairy farming, England.

Wheat farming, U.S.A.

Sheep farming, New Zealand.

In Britain it would be difficult to grow oranges outside, because you need long hours of sunshine to ripen them.

In the past, people could only buy food and materials from the farmers nearby.
It was difficult to move food a long way because it might go bad on the journey. Now we can freeze food which keeps it fresh. We also have better ways to move food so this means we can buy and use food from all over the world.

Banana growing, Trinidad.

Cotton growing, the Sudan.

Rice growing, south China.

Under the ground

Coal, oil, iron ore and clay are some of the minerals
we need, which must be dug out of the ground.
First someone has to work out just where
the minerals are. Then machinery must be bought.

The workers who do the mining and drilling need
special skills. Some must be strong to dig deep
into the earth. Others must learn how to use and
take care of complicated machines. The manager's
job is to decide where and how everyone can work best.

Work is dangerous underground. Rocks might fall,
or there could be flooding. Miners agree to
special rules to make the job as safe as possible.

**Special equipment is usually needed for digging
and drilling minerals. Lead, zinc, copper and
silver are mined here.**

There are many different kinds of jobs to be done on an oil rig. These men work on the drill floor.

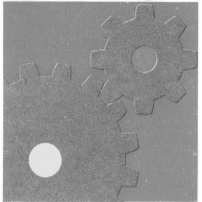

Working together

After the food has been grown, or the minerals dug up, people must work together to make them ready for us to use. On a production line many people will share this work. Each person does one small part of the work and then passes what they have done to the next worker. That person will add something and then pass it along again. This goes on, until what they are making is finished.

Working like this can be boring but workers depend on each other to keep the production line moving. Everyone is important.

Each group of workers is under a supervisor.
The supervisor's job is to make sure they work
quickly and without mistakes. Managers tell
the supervisors what to do and managers must
do what the people who own the factory want.

Workers often belong to trades unions.
They choose union leaders who will ask the
factory owners for the wages they want.
They also make sure the factory is a safe place
to work in. If the unions and the owners
can't agree, the workers might go on strike.
This means that they stop working. Then they won't
be paid by the factory, but the owners won't have
anything to sell either.

**Workers tell their
supervisor how work
on the line is going.**

**The supervisor reports
this to her manager.**

Using machines

Some workers make things we need from minerals. After iron ore has been dug from the ground, it is melted down and can be made into sheets of steel. Later the sheets may be used to make cars, cookers and aeroplanes. Oil may be changed into petrol but can also be turned into plastic for toys or records. Clay doesn't have to be changed very much before it is shaped and baked into bricks, cups and plates.

These jobs are often done in large factories, full of expensive and complicated machinery. Workers can make far more with machines than by working on their own with simple tools.

This potter can only make a few things in a day but each one is different. In a china factory, many more things are made that all look exactly the same.

Who owns the factory and machines?
They are not usually owned by the people
who work there. Some factories are owned by
the government and some are owned by people
who share the company between them.
They are called shareholders.

The owners have to buy the machines and
pay the workers. They sell the goods for
more money than it cost to make them.
The money left over is called the profit.

In this Japanese factory, cars are made by machines.
We call them robots.

On the move

Once, everyone lived near to their work.
They could walk to their fields or animals.
Some peasant farmers can still do this
but many people now have to travel to the place
where their work is needed.

Goods must be moved from where they are grown
or mined, to the factories. Before we can
buy anything, it must be moved again from
the factory to the warehouse and from
the warehouse to the shop.

People used to carry everything themselves,
or they would have an animal to help them.

**How many different transport routes
can you see in this picture?**

**These air traffic controllers plan
the movement of aeroplanes.**

Later canals were used to move heavy loads.
Railways could do this faster. Now lorries
can reach more places than trains.

Some things have to be carried across the world
to get to us. Britain imports things like rice,
bananas and cotton from other countries
and sends goods round the world to other
people. Goods are exported by road, rail,
sea and air. People have to plan where things
should be moved to and how best to move them.

For sale

This warehouse stores goods until they are needed in the supermarket.

It would be difficult for a factory or a farm to sell everything straight to us because we don't want to buy too much all at once. So lorry loads of goods are sent from the factory to a large building called a warehouse. Here they are stored until they are needed by the shops. Then we can decide how much we want to buy.

A factory might want to sell us a lorry load of toilet paper, or a tankerful of milk.

Shopkeepers have to sell things for more than
it cost to buy them from the factories.
The extra money pays for moving things to the shop,
the wages for the people who work in the shop,
the shop building and the profit for the owner.
The profit is the money left over when all this
has been paid for. This way, the shopkeeper has money
to buy food, clothes and somewhere to live too.

**Today supermarkets are very large and sell
many goods for the home. People can help
themselves instead of asking the
shop assistant for what they want.**

What else is work?

Think about it

Lots of people work hard without making anything at all! Their job is doing things for other people. They might look after us when we are ill, or they might teach us. Some people have to plan and make decisions about what other people will do.
They might help to make an office run smoothly. We cannot see what they have been working on until other people carry out their ideas.

architect

designer

composer

Fun for us

Nobody works all the time. When it is over,
most of us like to have fun or relax. Perhaps we go
to a football match, listen to music, read a book
or watch television.

But even this means that some people have to be
working. Someone has worked to write this book for you.
Other people have worked to draw the pictures and
take the photographs.

**It can be hard work making a television programme, even though
the people doing it seem to be enjoying themselves.**

What next?

By the time you are grown up there will probably
be new and different work to do. Jobs that people
used to do, are already being done by machines.
For instance, you have seen how machines can make
cars and dig up minerals. New machines using
the microchip, can do many jobs faster, better
and cheaper than people. A calculator can add up a
long sum much faster than you can in your head.

As machines do more and more, there will probably
be less work for people and some people may be
unemployed, unable to earn money.
But as machines do more of the work, people
will not have to work such long hours. We will all
have more spare time.

**These children have told the computer facts about
the jobs people did a hundred years ago. This machine
can remember them and sort them out very quickly.**

What might we do in this spare time?
Perhaps in the future there will be more jobs that
help people have fun and fewer jobs making things.

What would you like to do when you grow up?

6

Our Planet

Susan Baker

About this chapter

This chapter is about our planet, Earth, the huge rocky sphere we live on as it spins round the sun.

Where did our planet come from? Nobody knows for certain, but people have tried to work out how the sun and the planets may have been formed. Spaceships are exploring the other planets and telling us more about them, year by year.

Has our planet always looked the same? No, it has changed over and over again since it was formed millions of years ago. It is still changing because of what is going on inside it, and because of the weather. People are changing the Earth too, for better and for worse.

The sun and its family of planets and moons is called the solar system. Our sun is just one of the billions of stars in our galaxy.

The Earth seen from space.

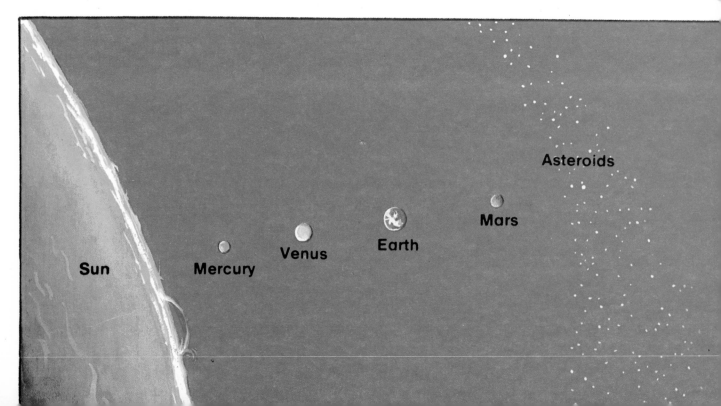

Sun Mercury Venus Earth Mars Asteroids

People go exploring underground, studying rocks and searching for minerals. Exploring caves is an exciting but dangerous sport.

Jupiter

Saturn

Uranus

Neptune

Pluto

The Earth is our planet

Land and sea

What can you see from your window – cars, houses, factories, trees, hills in the distance? Perhaps you can see a river on its way from the hills to the sea.

You are looking at just a tiny part of the planet we live on, which we call Earth. You may think that the Earth is flat, just as some people did long ago, but it is really a huge sphere, spinning through space.

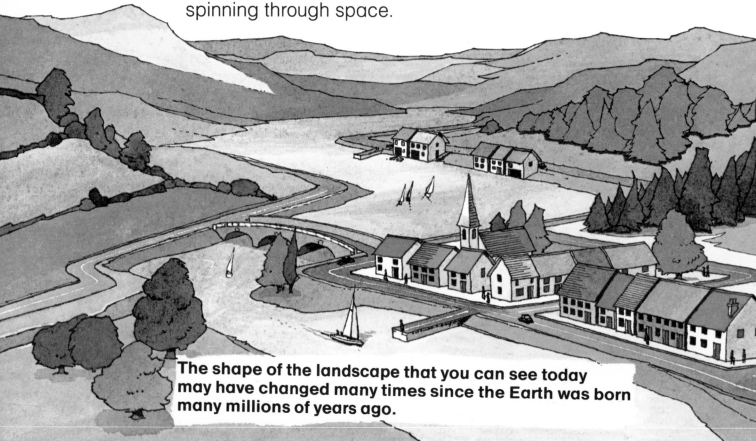

The shape of the landscape that you can see today may have changed many times since the Earth was born many millions of years ago.

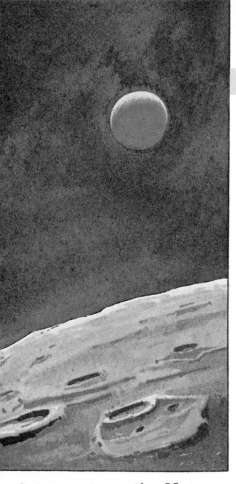

Astronauts on the Moon saw the complete globe shape of the Earth.

The Earth's rocky surface is just a thin shell called the crust. The surface has been carved into mountains and valleys. In some places there is a rich covering of soil, in others there are deserts of sand, rock or ice.

Nearly two thirds of the Earth's surface is covered with water. Under the sea, there is solid rock and sand.

For thousands of years people have dug deep into the Earth to take out minerals such as coal, oil, diamonds, and gold. From the rocks and minerals in the crust, we get raw materials. These are used for building houses and roads and for making all sorts of things, from teacups to cars.

The Earth also gives us some of the power we need to heat and light our homes and machines.

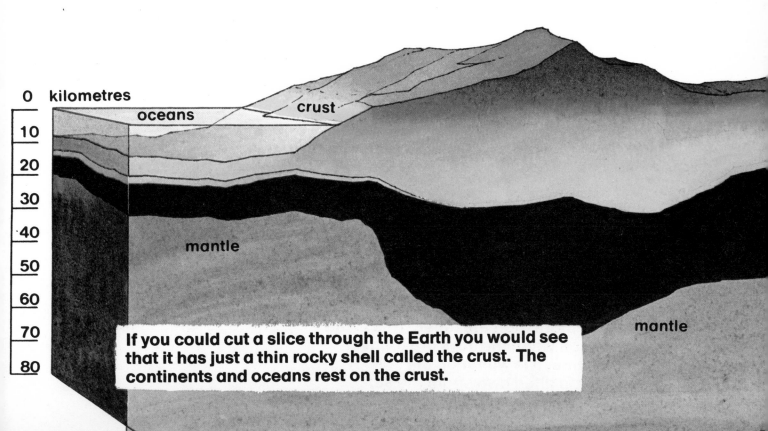

0 **kilometres**

oceans   **crust**

10

20

30

40   **mantle**

50

60

70   **mantle**

80

If you could cut a slice through the Earth you would see that it has just a thin rocky shell called the crust. The continents and oceans rest on the crust.

The Earth is a spinning top

Thousands of years ago, people thought
that the sun moved across the sky each day
while the Earth stayed still. But it is really
the Earth that is moving. It spins round like a top,
as if it had a great stick passing through
the middle. This imaginary stick is called the axis.
The ends of the axis are called the North and
South poles.

The Earth takes twenty four hours to complete
each full turn. While one half is facing the sun,
it is day time there. It is night time on the half
that is facing away from the sun. Out in space,
there is the twinkling light of billions of
other suns far, far away.
They are the stars.

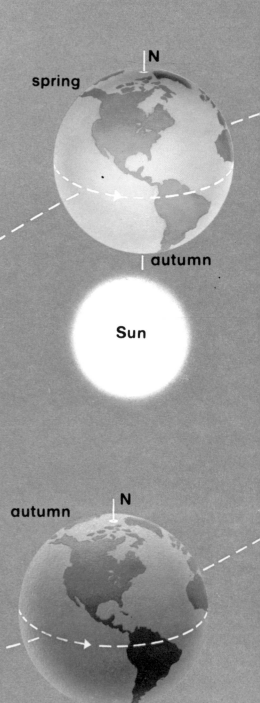

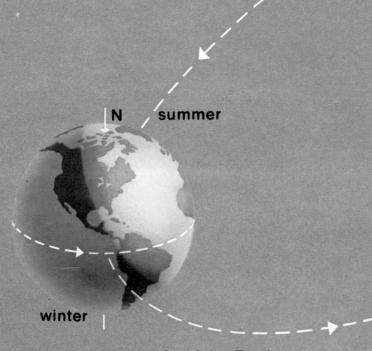

**For half the year one side of the Earth
faces the sun more than the other. This is the
summer season when the days are longest.
At the same time, it is winter on the side of
the Earth that is tilted away from the sun.**

The Earth moves round the sun while it spins on its axis. It takes one year of 365¼ days to travel right round the sun.

N winter

summer

According to a Greek legend, the sun drove a chariot with four horses across the sky each day.

In Britain, it is usually cold and wintry at Christmas and there may be snow.

In Australia, many people can have Christmas lunch outdoors, in the summer sun.

What is a planet?

Earth

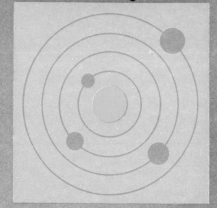

Sun

The solar system

When you look at the sun in the evening, does it sometimes look like a big red ball of fire?
All the stars are made mostly of burning gas which gives off a brilliant light. Our sun is just one of the millions of stars in our group or galaxy. There are millions of other galaxies in the universe.

There are explosions going on inside the fiery furnace of the sun all the time. The sun sends out powerful heat rays. We can feel the heat and see the light on our planet during the day.
A blanket of gases called the atmosphere protects the Earth from most of the harmful rays.

The nine planets of the solar system circle round the sun. A ball of rock we call the Moon circles round the Earth. Some of the planets have several moons.

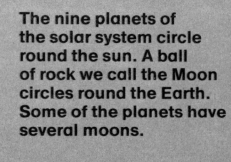

Jupiter and its moons

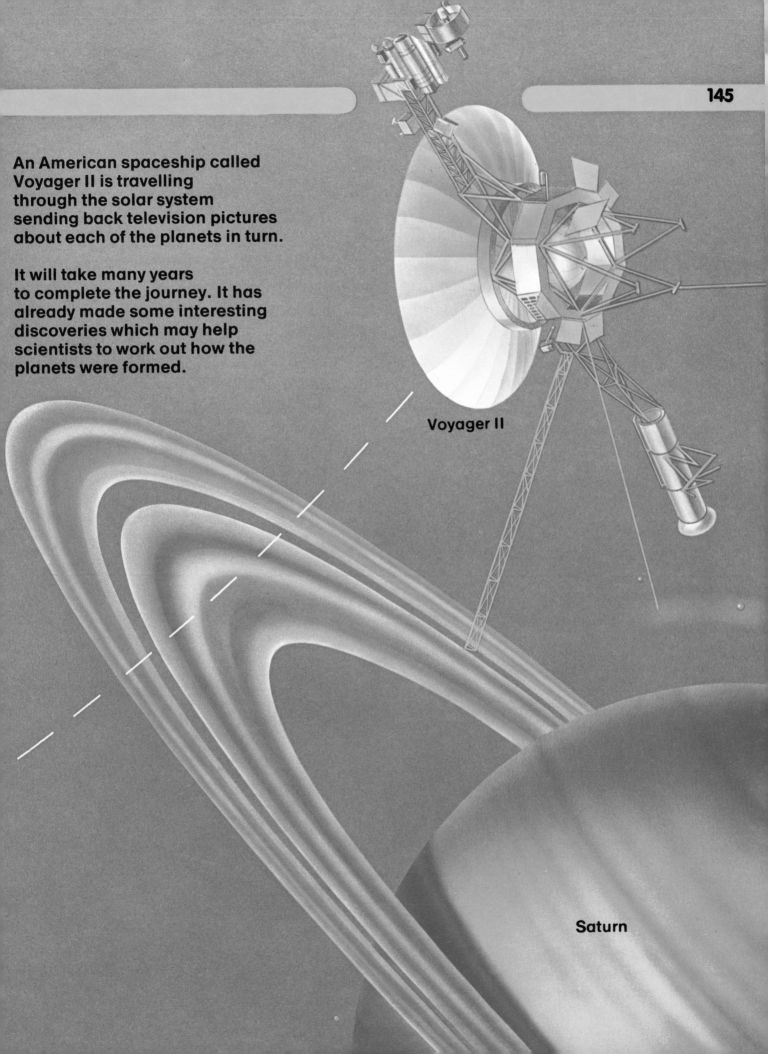

An American spaceship called Voyager II is travelling through the solar system sending back television pictures about each of the planets in turn.

It will take many years to complete the journey. It has already made some interesting discoveries which may help scientists to work out how the planets were formed.

Voyager II

Saturn

How the Earth began

No one is certain how, or when the planets were formed. Our star, the sun, was probably born in space when a great cloud of gas and dust collapsed in on itself and grew enormously hot.

There are nine planets and, like the Earth, they may have started as just a collection of gassy dust and rock whirling through the cloud round the sun. The new Earth gradually became a ball of melted rock. As it grew bigger and heavier, it cooled and a thin crust formed. All this took millions of years.

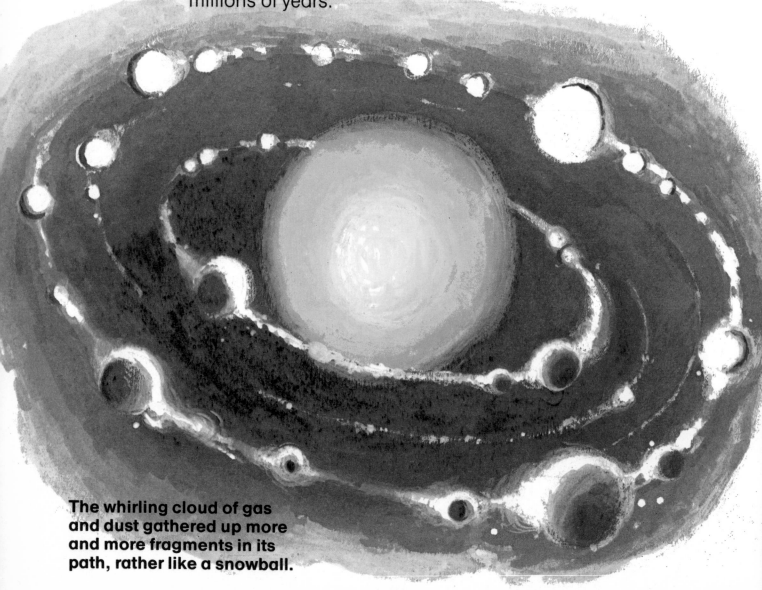

The whirling cloud of gas and dust gathered up more and more fragments in its path, rather like a snowball.

As the whirling cloud grew larger, the fragments were pressed together more and more tightly into a ball until they melted. Later a thin crust formed.

Huge chunks of rock from space, called meteorites, pierced through the Earth's crust and melted inside the Earth. The atmosphere formed slowly from the gas and steam sent up as the meteorites crashed into the Earth.

As the Earth cooled the steam turned to rain and the oceans were filled.

Hot rock underground

Only the thin crust of the Earth is hard and cold.
Inside, is the hot core surrounded by a
mantle of partly-melted rock.

The Earth's cold crust is made up of enormous plates
that fit together like a jigsaw. The plates rest
on the top of the mantle which moves continuously,
but very slowly, like boiling toffee.
It is the terrific heat and pressure inside
the Earth that keeps the mantle moving.

The mantle is gradually moving underneath
some of the plates, carrying them about very slowly.

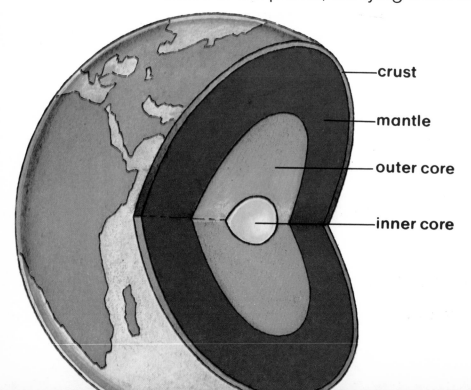

crust

mantle

outer core

inner core

**This shows what the inside
of the Earth is like.
The outside on which we
live is the crust. Beneath
is the mantle.
It is nearly 3000 km thick.
The centre of the Earth
is called the core.**

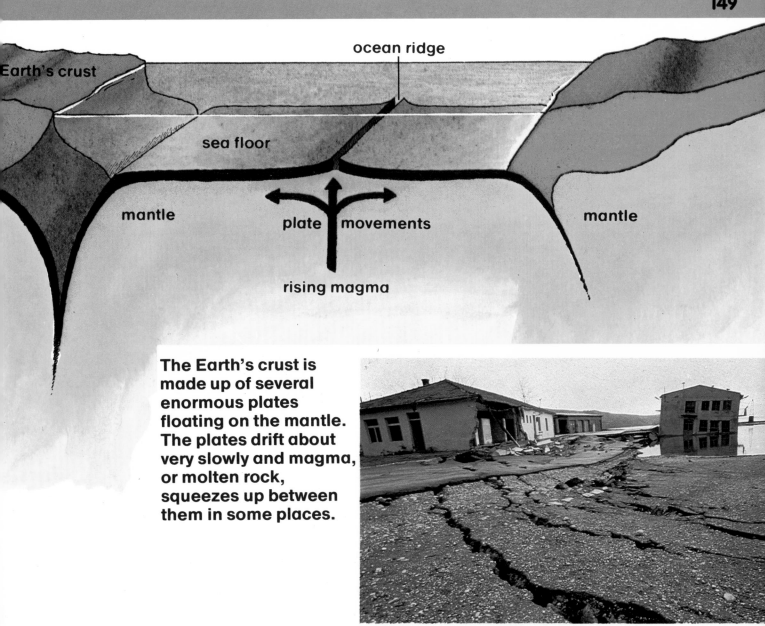

ocean ridge

Earth's crust

sea floor

mantle

plate movements

mantle

rising magma

The Earth's crust is made up of several enormous plates floating on the mantle. The plates drift about very slowly and magma, or molten rock, squeezes up between them in some places.

Each plate moves about on the Earth, perhaps only a few centimetres each year. Sometimes it touches another plate. Then the two plates press together until one of them is forced to dip down and slide beneath the other.

As the plates move, the rocks in the crust are squeezed or stretched. In some places, the rocks bend and buckle and slowly rise up to form high plains or mountains. All this takes millions of years.

As the plates move, the rocks above sometimes crack suddenly. The ground all round ripples and shakes and buildings collapse. This is called an earthquake.

How mountains were made

The youngest mountains on Earth began to rise up
millions of years ago, and they are still growing.
They began to form when some of the huge plates
collided with each other.

As one plate dips down and slides under another,
the rocks at the surface are pressed together
and push upwards to form ranges of mountains.
Huge slabs of rock crumple and fold up,
as if someone was pushing a cloth aside on a table.

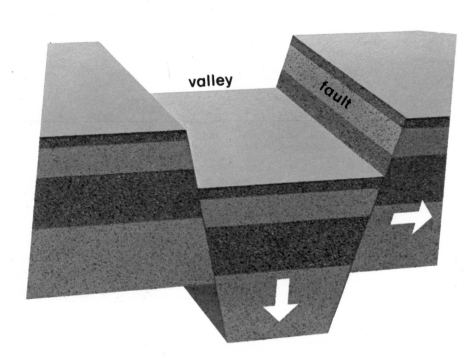

**When huge slabs of rock are folded,
the rock may crack under the enormous
strain and a complete block may shift
up, down or sideways. The line of the
crack is called a fault.**

The Himalayas are young
mountains which are still
rising up slowly. But
sun, wind, ice and snow are
wearing them down all the
time. The crumbled rock
fragments are carried away
in the muddy rivers.
The fragments may form
new sedimentary rock.

The rock folds at Lulworth Cove in England show up
layers of clay and limestone.

Volcanoes

Mountains built from the folded rock rise up very slowly, taking millions of years to form. But there are some mountains that can grow many metres in just a few days. These are the volcanoes.

Long ago, when the Earth was quite young, there must have been thousands of volcanoes pouring out fire, smoke and molten rock. Now there are only about 500 active volcanoes on Earth. The rest have become dormant, or 'gone to sleep'.

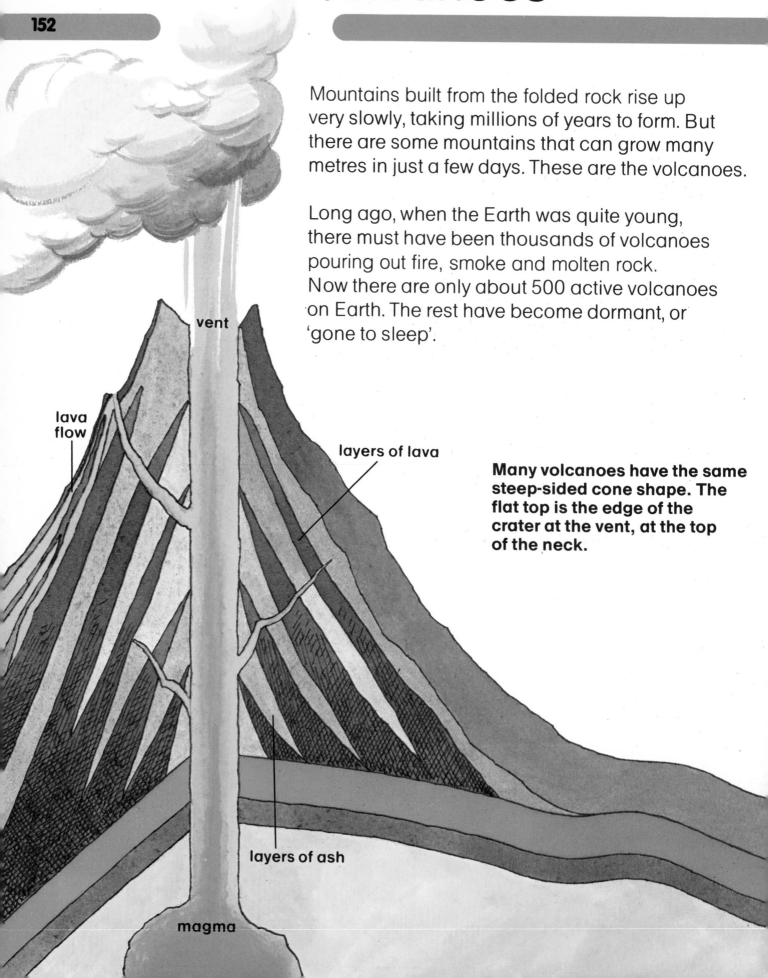

vent

lava flow

layers of lava

Many volcanoes have the same steep-sided cone shape. The flat top is the edge of the crater at the vent, at the top of the neck.

layers of ash

magma

There are many active volcanoes in the Pacific Ocean. They form the "ring of fire". Bursts of fire and rivers of lava like this one in Hawaii can be seen often.

After a volcano has burst or erupted, a small mound of cooling lava quickly grows round the crack or vent. A hill can form in a few weeks. The seething magma under the crust tends to find the same weak spot again and the same volcano may erupt again.

The next eruption is likely to be even more violent and dangerous if the magma is trapped for a long time. It builds enormous pressure under the hard plug of old magma blocking the vent. So showers of hot ash, burning gas and white hot lava burst out. Many people and animals have been taken by surprise and killed when a dormant volcano has erupted.

The rock factory

Crystal needles of the igneous rock quartz, bedded in a copper mineral.

If you look at the pebbles in a stream you may find many different kinds but they will all have been formed in one of the three different ways that rock is made.

You might find a smooth speckly lump of granite. Granite is one of the kinds of igneous rock. It is made from hot magma that has cooled under the crust.

The rock on the Earth's surface is slowly being worn away all the time. It crumbles finally into tiny pieces which are washed or blown away to different places.

A small slice of the metamorphic rock gneiss (pronounced nice). The name means sparkling.

This child is collecting pebbles of many different shapes and sizes.

Most of this rock ends up at the bottom
of the sea or lakes in sandy layers called sediments.
The layers of sediment get thicker and heavier until
they are pressed together hard enough to turn
into sedimentary rock, such as sandstone.

When hot magma pushes up under the crust,
the rocks nearby are heated and pressed enormously.
They may turn into the third kind of rock, called
metamorphic rock. Metamorphic means changed.
Crumbly limestone is turned into hard marble.
Soft, muddy shale is turned into hard, flaky slate.

**This fossil is the shape
in the rock of an
animal's shell.**

**People who study the rocks are called
geologists. They search for useful
kinds of rocks and minerals and work
out the history of the Earth. Fossils sometimes
give a clue about the age of the rock.**

The changing Earth

The weather

You can see how the weather is changing the world
a little every day. The little whirls of dust
in the street are blowing away precious soil.
After heavy rain, the water rushes into the
drains carrying mud, leaves and little stones. Murky
water in a stream carries silty sediments,
which may eventually find their way to the sea.
One day they will form into new sedimentary rock.

**Gale force winds have thrown sea water at the
cliffs with a load of sand and pebbles
and cut through a weak spot in the cliff.**

**This is a glacier. It is a huge river
of ice which flows very slowly.**

Windblown sand has carved this Californian desert rock into a strange shape.

As fast as the rocks are made, they are being worn away again. Rain, wind, ice and the heat of the sun all attack them. Look at the foot of any cliff and you will see a heap of broken rock, worn down by the weather or the sea.

The wind is an amazing sculptor, especially in the deserts. It heaps sand into ripples and hills called dunes and hurls it at the rocks with terrific force. The sand grinds and rubs the rocks into strange shapes.

People damage the Earth

Is the grass where you play all muddy and worn into bare patches? If it is, probably it is because too many people use it without giving it a chance to grow.

If farmers use their land in the wrong way by growing the wrong crops or using too much chemical fertiliser, the soil turns to dust. Then, the wind blows the dust away. Only thin, dry sand and rock are left and nothing will grow properly.

This bird was killed by oil spilled by a tanker off the coast of Brittany. Wherever people live they make a lot of dirt and rubbish.

This forest in South America has been cleared for farming. Cutting down too many trees destroys wild life and damages the soil. Without trees, the soil dries out and loses its goodness.

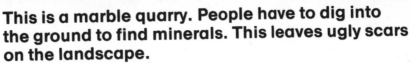

This is a marble quarry. People have to dig into the ground to find minerals. This leaves ugly scars on the landscape.

Only a small part of the Earth's crust is good farmland but there are millions of people who need food. People also need houses, roads and factories. The building materials and minerals for the factories come from inside the Earth. People dig quarries, mines and wells to find gravel, stone, metal, coal and oil. All this uses up more land.

Metals and minerals take millions of years to form in the Earth's crust, but some are being used up very quickly. If supplies of coal and oil run short we shall have to look for other sources of power.

A better planet?

People have ruined parts of the Earth. But look at
any piece of wasteland or ruined building
and you will see how nature is gradually
winning it back.

Streams wash themselves clean after a time
if no more dirt is put in them. The air grows clean
and clear again without smoke and fumes
from chimneys and cars.

Many people are trying to improve the Earth
by working more carefully and giving nature
a chance to repair the damage.

**This was a busy waterway a hundred
years ago. Weeds have now taken over
the site.**

**People have learned how to
survive on every part of
the Earth's rocky surface.
Now they are exploring,
working and living under
the sea too.**

Caring for nature in a US National Park.

Seas and Oceans

Ron Taylor

About this chapter

At one time or another, most of us visit the sea.
This happens when we go on our seaside holidays.
Of course, some people may never see the sea.
They live far from the oceans, in vast countries
such as Russia and China. The word ocean
is just another name for a very large sea.

In the seaside scene, the sea is calm.
But some seaside places have waves
like these.

Other people live close to the sea. Their homes are near seaside beaches, or on seaside cliffs. From their homes, they can look right out over the waves. Even from its edge, the sea looks very big. In fact, there is much more sea than land. This book tells you about all that sea.

seaweed

beadlet anemones

periwinkles

sea lettuce

limpets

mussels

sea snail

keelworm tubes

These children have discovered many forms of life on the sea shore.

starfish

crab

barnacles

Seaside holidays

Along the coast there are many holiday towns.
Some of these have been famous for centuries.
The picture shows a large English seaside town,
about eighty years ago. The town still looks
something like this, even today.

Of course, the style of clothes has changed.
Another difference is the bathing machines
on the beach. These were huts on wheels,
in which bathers changed their clothes.
What other differences can you see?

bathing machine

Harbour towns

Many harbour towns are thousands of years old.
Long ago, they were visited by sailing ships
carrying many different cargoes. Nowadays,
the biggest harbours are visited by modern
ocean liners, cargo ships and oil tankers.
Harbours today still contain sailing
boats. But these boats are now used mainly
for pleasure sailing, not for cargo carrying.

Important ships' cargoes include all kinds
of foods. They also include clothing,
machinery and fuels such as coal and oil.
And of course, people travel by ship, too.

**A dock is a place inside
a harbour where ships can
load and unload their
cargoes.**

**A small harbour is often very pretty.
Some small harbour towns are
favourite seaside holiday places.**

Some seaside towns have harbours and docks.
A harbour is a safe place for ships and boats.
Many harbours are natural bays, or inlets
in the coastline. Often, a sea wall is built
across the mouth of the harbour. This helps
to keep the sea smooth and safe inside
the harbour, even when it is very rough outside.

A dock is a place inside a harbour, where ships
can load and unload their cargoes. Many cargoes
of food arrive from abroad. In return, cargoes
of machinery may leave for abroad. In some docks
ships full of passengers arrive or leave regularly.

**Hong Kong has a big harbour in which
thousands of people live. Their floating
homes are sailing boats called sampans
and junks.**

Out at sea

Boats and sailors

Boats and ships are used for travel on the sea.
Ship is the name for a large boat. At one time,
most boats travelled using the power of the wind.
They used their sails to 'catch the wind'.
Nowadays, most ships travel by engine power,
but sailors still often use sailing boats.
They sail in them for sport, or even race them
right across the oceans.

**This sailor is sailing her dinghy
back into harbour. She sails between the
pole markers, where the water is deep enough.**

**Cutty Sark is a famous sailing ship.
She is one of the fast clippers that
carried cargoes of tea across the world,
one hundred years ago. But Cutty Sark
is now a museum ship at Greenwich, London,
visited by thousands of people each year.**

Sailing boats have various names. A dinghy
is a very small sailing boat. A yacht is larger
and a clipper is larger still.

In dinghies, sailors sail only near the coast.
Small boats sometimes capsize in rougher water.
For ocean races, sailors use larger yachts.
Clippers once sailed right around the world.
These large, fast sailing ships carried
important cargoes, such as tea.

**A small boat quickly gets
out of the way, as a big
tanker looms up.**

Today's cargo ships are bigger than clippers.
Powerful engines carry them around the world.

Far out at sea

The sailors on this raft are many thousands of kilometres out at sea. This famous raft is named Kon Tiki. Its long voyage lasted for more than three months. You can see how far it travelled, from the map.

Unlike boats, rafts are flat. But like a boat, a raft can travel by sail. On a raft, a sailor is very near the sea surface. He can see everything in the water. On their long voyage, Kon Tiki sailors saw many strange sea creatures, such as flying fishes.

The sailors of Kon Tiki on their floating home. They last saw dry land a month ago. It will be 2 months more before they finish their voyage.

Pacific Ocean

Kon Tiki sailed for 3 months. In all this time, it crossed only a part of the vast Pacific Ocean.

Swimmers and floaters

Many creatures live near the sea surface.
The largest sea creatures include many fishes.
Large fishes are often the strongest swimmers.

Other sea creatures are very small indeed.
They go usually wherever the sea carries them,
so that mainly, they are floaters. Plankton is
the name for all this tiny floating life. You can see
some small creatures of the plankton in the picture
below. They are called copepods. Countless
millions of copepods live near the sea surface.

diver

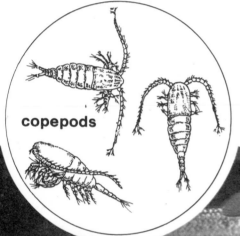

copepods

**Herring are fast swimmers.
These small fishes feed
on even smaller copepods,
shown inside the circle.
In turn, herring are food
for bigger fishes.**

marlin

tuna

shark

The marlin, tuna and shark are large, fast swimmers. They chase and catch smaller fishes for food.

Jellyfishes are weak swimmers. They often go where the strong sea pushes them. So they are floaters too.

Copepods feed on tiny plants that grow in the sunlit part of the sea. The sun helps these tiny plants to make all the food they need to live. In turn, the plants produce oxygen. This is a vital part of the air that animals need to stay alive.

Small sea animals are often food for larger ones. For example, tiny copepods are eaten by small fishes. In turn, these are eaten by large fishes, such as sharks. But the largest sea creatures, the rorqual whales, feed off some of the smallest. They filter these out from the plankton, as they swim along.

Down in the sea

Warm and cold seas

Seas, like countries, can be cold or warm.
Near to the North Pole and the South Pole,
seas and oceans are usually cold. Near to the
Equator, seas and oceans are usually warmer.

Cold and warm seas both contain lots of life.
In cold, polar seas live many whales and seals.
Giant whales are the biggest of all animals.
In warm, tropical seas are the coral reefs.
Corals are composed of lots of small sea animals.
These are food for many colourful coral fishes.

**By the icy waters of the Antarctic Ocean, this elephant seal enjoys a lazy life.
His thick coat of fat protects him from the cold.**

In the warm coral sea swim butterfly and damsel fishes.
In the small picture, the little cleaner fish prepares to
clean out the mouth of a badger fish.

The ocean deeps

Deep down, the oceans are cold and dark. Light and warmth from the sun reaches down only a few hundred metres. But the deepest seas reach down as much as eight kilometres.

About fifty years ago, explorers first went down into the deeper seas. They travelled in special strong deep-sea craft. Using powerful lights, they saw strange fishes and other sea creatures in the cold dark waters. Some deep sea creatures are luminous. That is, parts of their bodies are brightly lit up.

A large sea spider crawls along the sea bed.

A deep sea anglerfish attracts a prawn with its brightly shining lure – then snaps the prawn up!

squid

The gulper eel is a weird deep sea fish.

Deep down in the sea, a sperm whale captures a large squid. Sperm whales often bear the scars of squid suckers, from deep sea fights.

The picture shows a very deep part of the ocean. In some places, the distance from top to bottom can be greater than the height of the tallest mountain. However, modern deep sea craft can explore even these deep, dark regions.

The work of the sea

Tides and waves

Sometimes the sea is very still and calm.
At other times, the sea is rough or choppy.
Then, sea water moves up and down in waves.

Mostly, ocean waves are caused by the wind.
In a bad storm, the wind can make huge waves. When
volcanoes burst or erupt, they can cause giant waves.
Earthquakes can also cause giant waves. But this
happens only rarely. Sometimes, a boat or ship
is wrecked in a storm. Then, a lifeboat may put out,
to save human lives.

In some seaside places, the rise and fall of the tide can be 10 metres or more.

**A modern lifeboat is powerful and safe.
Lifeboat people make rescues even in rough seas.
But the sea can be so dangerous
that their lives are still at risk.**

As you walk along the shore you will notice
that the water line is not always in the same place.
The tide comes in and goes out. This happens
about twice each day. When the tide comes in, sea
water rises higher. When the tide goes out, sea
water sinks lower.

Tides are caused by the Sun and Moon pulling
by gravity on the Earth's water.

Sea water can also move in a broad stream.
These streams are the ocean currents. They flow
both on the sea surface and deeper down.

**Waves and spray
wear away cliffs.
Here at Durdle Door, Dorset,
they have worn a door shape.**

Fishermen

Oceans are like vast larders, full of food.
Human beings have always enjoyed sea food.
The first people to eat sea food lived close
by the sea shore. They caught fishes with spears
and with small nets. In many parts of the world,
village fishermen still fish in this way.

Nowadays, most of the fishes we eat are caught
from boats, such as fishing trawlers.
Much larger nets are used, to make bigger catches.

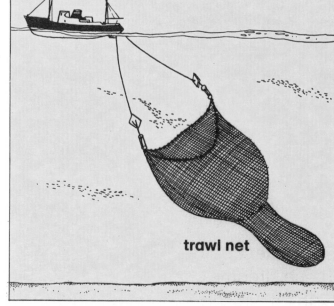

trawl net

**Over the side of their trawler, fishermen
pull many a tumbling catch of silvery
fishes. Right: a trawl net can catch a
whole large shoal of fishes.**

In this Asian seaside village, a boat has carried out a fishing net. Now, the villagers haul in the net by its long ropes. The result will be a small but precious catch of fishes.

A village fisherman, with his small net, will catch one or two fishes at a time. But a fishing trawler, with its big net, may catch thousands at a time.

The trawler may bring back many tonnes of fishes to be sold at the dockside of a fishing town. Or, the trawler may take its big catch of fishes to a mother ship. This is a very large ship, on which thousands of fishes are frozen. This way, the fishes stay fresh for a much longer time. But fleets of trawlers and their mother ships catch so many fishes, that some kinds are dying out.

Delicious seafood includes crabs and lobsters. These are caught usually in baskets or "pots".

Smaller prawns and shrimps are caught with nets. Octopuses and squid also make very tasty sea food.

Ocean riches

As we have seen already, the seas provide
vast amounts of food. In some countries,
more fish is eaten than any other kind of flesh food.
In hot countries, the fish is often first dried in
the sun. It keeps better, this way.

In colder seas, whales are often hunted
by Japanese and Russian fishermen.
Whale meat is a popular food in Japan.
Also, whale oil is used, for example, in cosmetics.
But so many whales have been hunted and killed
that some kinds are now very rare.
Many people want whale hunting stopped altogether.

Rows of fishes hang up to dry in the sun.
Dried fish is a favourite food
in many hot countries, where fish
otherwise goes bad rather quickly.

Beneath the ocean bed are oil, gas and minerals.
Petroleum oil and natural gas are valuable fuels.
We use them to heat homes and factories, and also
to power engines and other machines.

To get at these fuels, engineers on drilling rigs
drill deep down below the ocean floor.
Valuable minerals, such as coal and metals,
can also be mined, on or below the sea floor.
But the harvesting of ocean riches also has
a bad side. Modern over-fishing uses up
all the food fishes. Mining the sea bed also
dirties, or pollutes the sea.

**Huge floating rigs, such as
this one, explore and drill
the ocean floor to obtain
valuable fuel oil and gas.**

**Death of a school of whales. Whales have long
been hunted for their flesh and oil.
As a result, some kinds of whales unfortunately
are now very rare and may soon die out altogether.**

Sea treasure

Divers sometimes search for treasure in the sea.
This treasure includes gold and silver, carried
by ships that were wrecked and sunk long ago.

Spanish galleons were among these great wooden ships.
They brought back precious metals from America.
Or, the gold and silver might be pirate treasure,
perhaps plundered from the great treasure ships.

Pirates are well-known robbers of sea treasure.
Sir Francis Drake was a famous navy captain
who was also a pirate. He robbed Spanish galleons
of their treasure, for England and Queen Elizabeth 1.

**A diver brings up a vase from
a sunken ship.**

Barbarossa was a Turkish pirate who robbed many ships of their treasure.

More sea treasure once belonged to ancient towns and cities, now covered by the sea.
Divers take many risks to bring up this treasure.
It is then shown off in museums.

Sometimes, a whole ship can be brought up as sea treasure. For example, several long boats of the famous Viking sea warriors have been brought up whole. The large picture on this page shows how an even bigger war ship sank, at the Battle of Portsmouth. After 437 years on the cold sea bed, the Mary Rose was raised to the surface.

In Portsmouth in 1545, French ships, left, and English ships, right, prepared for battle. But in the centre, the Mary Rose was sinking.

8

Life on Earth

Cathy Kilpatrick

About this chapter

Do you have pet animals? Are there plants in your school or house or garden? Plants and animals can make our lives more fun and they make the world more colourful.

But we also need plants and animals to give us food. Some animals do work for us. Plants make the part of the air, called oxygen, that we breathe.

People live all over the world. There are different plants and animals in all the different places people live in.

grasses

moss

lichen

spider

earwig

thrush

slug

woodlice

snail

Even around a small rock you can find all sorts of wildlife. Where else can you find plants and animals?

In this market you can see many of the ways in which plants and animals are important to us. There are lots of fruit, vegetables, fish and meat which we eat. There are animals which work for us.

The living world

Life around you

You are living; so are your family, friends and pets. Are flowers and vegetables in gardens living? All living things feed, grow and make new living things.

Look around you to see what is living and what is not. You should be able to see lots of both. Anything not alive is called non-living. Trees are living, but from the trees we get non-living wood.

There are both plants and animals here. There are also some non-living things. How can you tell the difference?

This plant is yellow and drooping. This happens when plants do not get enough sunlight and water.

Both plants and animals need water to survive. Most plants have roots that take water and minerals from the soil. Animals drink water.

As well as water, plants need sunlight. This gives plants energy so they can make leaves and other new plant material.

Animals need the sun for different reasons. We need it for warmth and for light to see by. We cannot make new material in the same way as plants. We must eat plants or other animals to get energy so that we can live and grow.

Pet animals need more care than plants. We have to give them food as well as water. If we give plants special things called fertilisers, they grow better.

Desert wildlife

Animals and plants live all over the Earth. They live in forests and grasslands. There is even wildlife in places like the deserts. In hot deserts there is too much sunlight and very little water. Other deserts can be much colder than a deep freeze.

Most plants and animals would die if they were put into deserts. But plants and animals can live there because they have the right shape and right way of life for the place they live in. We say they are adapted for survival.

In the hot deserts of Mexico, many animals hide in the sand to escape the heat of the day.

The barrel cactus has lots of ridges to give extra room to store water. Its roots spread out to get water.

rattlesnake

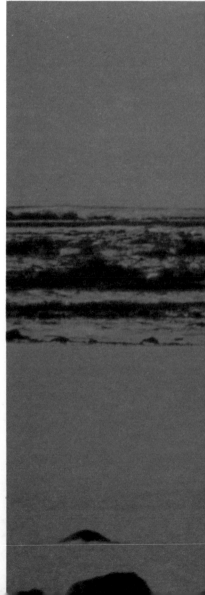

Adelie penguins feed on the shrimps of the Antarctic ocean. They build their nests from stones and they will cross 80 kilometres of ice to find them.

The polar bear's thick fur helps it
to survive the cold of the Arctic.
The only plants which can live there are
small and tough like grasses
and mosses.

Forests and grasslands

gibbons

creeper

tarsier

fern

tapir

Have you noticed that there are different kinds of tree in forests? Some trees lose all their leaves in autumn. These are the broad-leaved, or deciduous, trees. Oak trees and elm trees are deciduous. Other trees do not lose all their leaves at once. Instead, they lose a few at a time all through the year. These are evergreen trees. Pine trees and fir trees are evergreen.

In the hot places near the Earth's equator are the rain forests. Sometimes we call them jungles. Many plants grow close together there.

Jungles are the areas with the most animals and plants. This is because there is warmth, water and lots of food all the year round.

Every continent has areas of grassland. This is usually between the forests and the deserts. Grasslands have less rainfall than forests but are not as dry as deserts.

Grasslands are the homes of herds of grazing animals like the kangaroos of Australia and the wildebeeste of Africa. In America there are no longer many herds of bison, mainly because people have taken the grasslands for farming. Nearly all the bison were killed but now some survive in protected parks. Elephants live in the grasslands of Africa and India.

orchid

Gazelles and striped zebra live on the grasslands in Africa. There are few trees or other plants apart from the grass.

The world of animals

Useful animals

Many of us keep animals in our homes as pets. But some animals are not just friends, they are also helpful to us in other ways. For thousands of years, animals have done hard work for people. They are used mainly to move heavy loads or for people to ride.

We keep some animals as pets. They are fun to play with. They also need to be looked after.

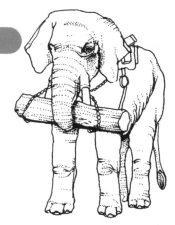

Elephants are used for moving heavy loads.

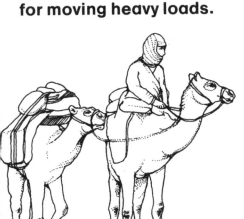

In the desert, camels carry people and goods.

Horses are still used for ploughing in some places. Other animals, such as oxen, may be used instead.

In rich countries where people can afford to buy trucks, cars and tractors, animals are now not used much for work. But in poor countries, they are still very important for farm work and travel.
Animals are also the main way to travel in countries without many roads or railways. In the Arctic, reindeer still pull sledges.

Animals provide us with milk, meat and wool. What other things do we get from animals?

All the animals which work for us are used to being with people. They are tame. We have to give them food because they cannot search for it. Animals which live in the wild find their own food.

Dogs can be trained to work. These sheepdogs are herding sheep in Australia. Some dogs help blind people.

The bumpy bone that runs all the way down the middle of your back is called a backbone. When you stroke cats or dogs you can probably feel their backbones. The backbone is the main part of your skeleton, which holds you up.

But some animals do not have backbones. Many of these are very simple kinds of animals. Some of them lived on Earth in prehistoric times, long before there were any people. Slugs are very soft animals without backbones. Snails have no backbones and are soft like the slugs but they have hard shells to protect them.

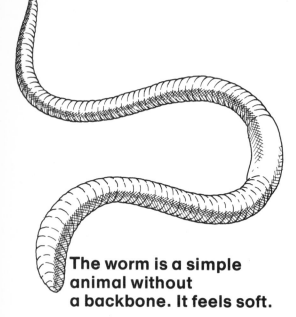

The worm is a simple animal without a backbone. It feels soft.

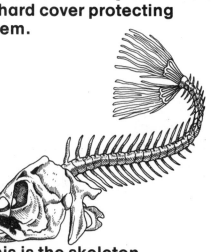

Ladybirds have no backbone or skeleton. They do have a hard cover protecting them.

This is the skeleton of a fish. You can see the backbone. Snakes, frogs and birds also have backbones.

Human babies need to be looked after for many years. Babies can feed on the milk which their mothers make.

Once this moth has laid
her eggs, she leaves
them. Caterpillars
will hatch from the eggs.
They will change in stages
until they become moths.

These are baby turtles
hatching. The turtles
have to make the dangerous
journey to water
without any help
from their parents.

Animals may be different from each other
in many more ways. All animals can make new animals
but they do not all produce them in the same way.

When you were born, you came out of your mother's
body. Some fishes give birth to baby fishes. But
most fishes lay eggs. A baby fish hatches
from each egg. Many other kinds of animal,
such as frogs, snakes and birds, also lay eggs.
Other very tiny and simple animals make new animals
by splitting their bodies. This produces two new animals
which look exactly the same as each other.

Animal groups

How many different kinds of animal do you think
there are in the world? Living on land and
in lakes, rivers and seas there are more than
one million different sorts of animal.

To make it easier to learn about animals,
scientists have divided them into groups.
Animals within a group are the same in many ways.
Some of the main groups of animals are the insects,
arachnids, fishes, reptiles, amphibians, birds,
mammals and various kinds of worm.

**A cow belongs to the group of animals
called mammals. So do people. Mammals
can feed their babies with their milk.
The milk is made by their bodies.**

humming bird

tiger moth

Birds have feathers
and lay their eggs in nests.
Many feed the young
birds until they are
able to leave the nest.

This moth is an insect.
Many young insects
go through some changes
before they become
adults. Adult insects have
6 legs.

garden orb spider

Spiders are arachnids.
These all have 8 legs.
Scorpions also belong
to the arachnid group.

midwife
toad

Crocodiles belong to
the group called reptiles.
Snakes, turtles, tortoises
and lizards are all reptiles.
Reptiles do not need
to lay their eggs in water.

Toads, frogs and newts
are all amphibians.
They like damp places
and usually lay their eggs
in water, so this toad
is unusual. Tadpoles
hatch from the eggs.

Helpful and harmful

Sometimes people eat cereal and milk for breakfast. Cereals come from the seeds of one group of plants called grasses. These grasses are carefully grown by farmers so that the seeds are large. They include wheat, oats, rice and maize.

We use plants in many ways — for food, building, fuels and medicines. But not all plants are useful. Some plants harm us. Have you ever been stung by a nettle? Other plants can make you ill.

parasol mushroom

fly agaric

Maize is used to feed animals and people eat it too. Corn oil comes from maize.

Some mushrooms and toadstools are poisonous. The parasol mushroom is safe to eat. The red colour of the fly agaric warns us that it is dangerous.

Foxglove leaves contain a poison. But it can be usefu From this poison is made a medicine for heart disease

Laburnums are related to peas but their seeds are poisonous.

Rubber trees grow in Africa, Asia and South America. People collect the white sap that oozes out when the bark is cut. Rubber is made from this.

The seed pods of the cotton plant burst open to show masses of white fibres. These are used to make cotton material.

Rice is grown mainly in Asia, in flooded fields. It is the main food of half the people in the world.

Why we need plants

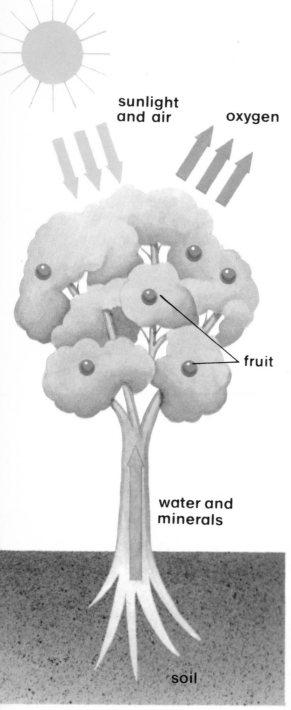

sunlight and air

oxygen

fruit

water and minerals

soil

What would the world be like without any plants?
It would not look as pleasant if there were
no flowers or trees. More importantly, people
and all the other animals would starve.
Most of what we eat, and what other animals eat,
comes from plants.

Only plants can make food directly. With the help of
sunlight they make the food from water and
part of the air. While they are making food,
plants also produce oxygen.
This is the part of the air that we use when we breathe
We need plants to keep life going on Earth.

**Through its roots, this
tree is taking in water
and minerals from the
soil. In the leaves,
air acts on the water.
From these, with
the help of sunlight,
food is made.**

**Plant leaves sometimes move to face the sun.
In the longer days of spring, they get
more sunlight. Then they can make more food
and new material and so plants grow.**

Producing new plants

Many plants have flowers at some time during the year. Flowers are special shoots which help some plants to make new plants. Part of the flower becomes the fruit. Inside the fruit is the seed. Bulbs are another way of making new plants. Plants such as daffodils and tulips grow from bulbs.

Why do fruits have so many different shapes? They are all made so that the seeds will be carried away from the parent plant. If this did not happen, there would be too many seeds in one place and they would not be able to grow.

Dandelion fruits have small parachutes. Because of these, the wind can scatter the seeds.

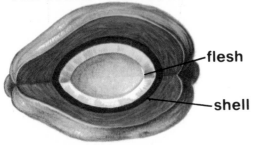

flesh

shell

inside a coconut

Birds help to scatter seeds. This bird eats the hawthorn berries and the hard seeds pass out in the bird's droppings.

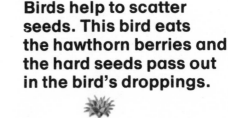

The coconut has one of the largest seeds in the world. Its light shell makes it float so that it can be carried away by water.

Buttercup fruits have small hooks on their tips. These catch on the fur of animals so that the seeds are carried away.

Changing wildlife

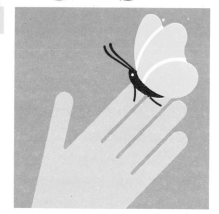

Life in the past

People used to believe that living things on Earth had always been the same. Today we know that the Earth is many millions of years old and that the plants and animals have changed in that time. Some living things died out because they were not able to survive when the climate changed or the land and sea changed. However, some plants and animals always survived and slowly changed to suit the new conditions.

Pteranodon

cycad

palm

fern

Brachiosaurus

Tyrannosaurus rex

Ichthyosaurus

ammonite

By studying fossils we can imagine how plants and animals looked in prehistoric times. There were no people then to write about what the Earth was like.

We can find out about plants and animals
of the past by studying rocks. Through the ages,
some land has slowly been worn away by seas and rivers.
In other places mud and soil have been built up
over the years to make new layers.

Sometimes a plant or animal was trapped
in these layers and the remains can still be seen
in the rocks. These remains are called fossils.
Fossils may be a footprint, a part of an animal's
skeleton, or the outline of a plant or animal.
Sometimes a whole animal is found. A woolly
mammoth's body was found frozen in Siberian ice
and it had been there 25,000 years.

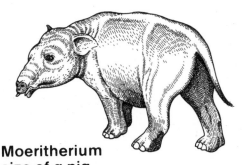

**Moeritherium
size of a pig**

**Since mammmals appeared
on Earth, there have been
many which looked like
the elephant.**

**Gomphotherium
2 metres long**

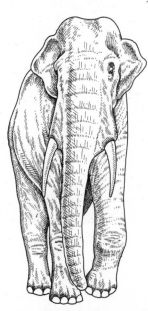

**Platybelodon
scooped up plants**

**Deinotherium
3 metres high**

Indian elephant

Wildlife in danger

All over the world hundreds of different kinds of plant and animal are in danger of dying out for ever. Thousands of plants and animals have died out naturally as time passed because of the changes on the Earth. However, in the last 150 years, it is mainly people that have put much of our wildlife in danger.

There are now many more people living on Earth than ever before. Land is needed for buildings and roads for all these people. Even more land is used for growing foods or rearing farm animals. Forests an natural grasslands have been cleared to make farmland. The wildlife which was there has gone.

There are many beautiful orchids in the world's jungles. As the jungles are cleared for farmland, the orchids die out.

Dumping rubbish and waste kills wildlife. This water has been poisoned so that the fish have died.

Before there were farms, wild animals were hunted for food and clothing. When guns were invented, killing animals became very easy. Large numbers have been killed for sport or for clothes, as well as for food. Elephants and walruses have been killed for their valuable ivory teeth. Some people use animal skins to decorate their homes.

Some plants and animals are pests. Sometimes poisons are used to get rid of them. However, many of these poisons may drain into lakes, rivers and seas. What happens to the animals living there?

Gorillas have become rare because their forest homes in Africa have been cleared. They climb into trees at night for safety. They sleep there in nests made from twisted branches and leaves.

Saving our wildlife

Many people are very worried about our wildlife. People who try to save animals and plants from dying out are called conservationists. Around the world there are many groups who want to conserve and protect our wildlife. One group is the World Wildlife Fund. Another, called Greenpeace does lots of work including protecting the whales.

There are many ways we can all help to save wildlife. Always get rid of rubbish in the right place. Broken glass can cut animals and they can choke on waste paper or string. Perhaps you could join a club to save wildlife.

buddleia

willowherb

wild oats

blackberry

nettle

Growing some of these plants in the corner of a garden gives animals food. You can watch the animals that come to feed.

Cleaning up ponds is something that you might be able to do in your area. You must have a grown-up in charge of you. Ask at your library about conservation groups.

The panda is the symbol
of the World Wildlife Fund.
Pandas are in danger
but some are safe in zoos.
Many animals live, protected,
in parks and zoos.

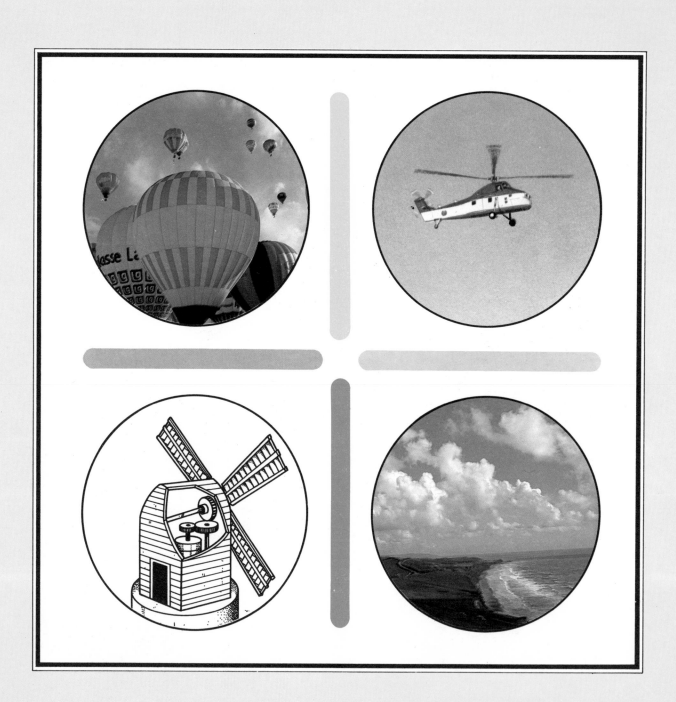

9

Into the Air

Robin Kerrod

About this chapter

All around us is something we can sometimes feel, but we cannot see it and we cannot taste it. It is the air. The air is one of the most important things on Earth. Without the air there would be no blue sky, no weather, no plants, no animals, no people. Beyond the air is space.

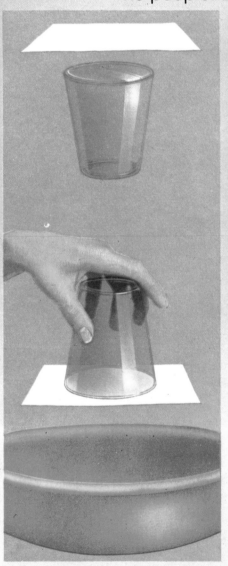

From space, the Earth looks blue. You are seeing our sky from the other side.

balloon

bird

clouds

You can show that the air presses on things. A piece of card keeps water in a glass because of air pressure. Do this carefully, over a bowl.

satellite

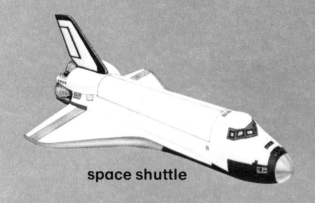

space shuttle

clouds

jet plane

helicopter

clouds

**Clouds form and birds fly
in the lower part of the air. Planes
like Concorde fly much higher up.
Spacecraft fly above the air, in space.**

What does the air do?

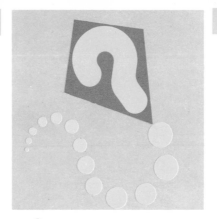

The air protects us

The air has no colour and no smell. It is a gas, or rather a mixture of gases. The main gases in the air are nitrogen, oxygen and water vapour.

The most important gas in the air is oxygen. Most living things need to breathe oxygen to stay alive. Without the oxygen in the air, Earth would be a dead world.

The Moon is dull, dry and dead. It has no atmosphere, so there is no life there.

If the Earth did not have an atmosphere, it would not be colourful and alive.

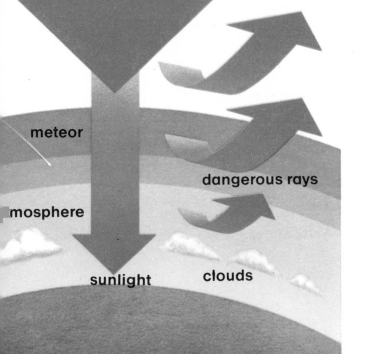

Sun

Sun's rays

meteor

mosphere

sunlight

clouds

dangerous rays

Scientists call the layer of air around the Earth the atmosphere. It protects us in many ways. It acts like a blanket and stops the Earth getting too cold at night when the Sun sets.
The atmosphere also stops dangerous rays reaching us from the Sun.

The atmosphere shields us from most of the rocks coming from outer space. These rocks are travelling so fast that they burn up in the atmosphere, and we see them as fiery streaks in the night sky.
We call these streaks meteors, or shooting stars.

The Earth's atmosphere protects us from many dangers. It keeps out extra heat and harmful rays from the Sun that would otherwise burn us.

This crater is one kilometre across and was made by a huge rock falling from space. It crashed to Earth about 20,000 years ago.

Air brings the weather

We can feel the air when it moves. It is the wind.
Winds blow all over the Earth as great masses of
air move from place to place. The kind of weather
we have depends on where these air masses have
come from. The air masses have such a big effect
on the weather because they carry with them water
in the form of an invisible gas, or vapour.

The weather changes day by day and usually
season by season. Every place on Earth has its own
weather pattern throughout the year.
We call this the climate.

Sun's heat

clouds

clouds

rain

water
vapour

water
vapour

lake

river

se

water drains
away
underground

**Water moves between the ground and the atmosphere
all the time. This is the water cycle. Water vapour
cools and forms water drops in clouds. When the
drops get large, they fall back to Earth as rain.**

Clouds can tell us a lot about the weather. Fluffy white cumulus clouds mean good weather.

Wispy cirrus clouds form very high in the sky. They usually mean fine weather.

Stratus clouds are grey and very low in the sky. If they stay, then rain is coming.

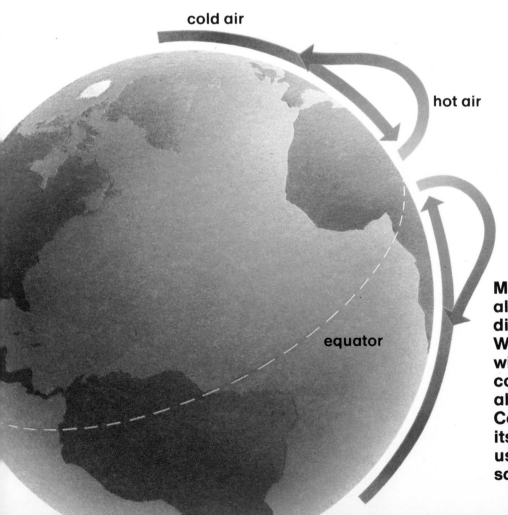

cold air

hot air

Sun's heat

equator

Many winds blow nearly always from the same direction over the Earth. We call them prevailing winds. Air over the hot countries near the equator also gets hot and rises. Cold air moves in to take its place. So the winds usually move in the same patterns.

The weather forecast

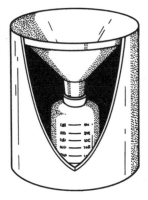

**rain gauge
measures rainfall**

The weather often changes rapidly. It may be fine and warm early in the morning, but cold and stormy by the afternoon. We all want to know what the weather will be like, to plan ahead.

To some people, knowing about future weather can be a matter of life and death. In some parts of the world, destructive blizzards and floods can occur. Many lives can be saved if people can be warned in advance. Farmers, airline pilots and ships' captains need to know about weather.

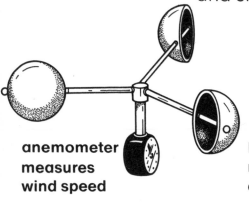

**anemometer
measures
wind speed**

**barometer
measures
air pressure**

drought

**These weather instruments
are some of those most
often used.**

**thermometer
measures how
hot or cold air is**

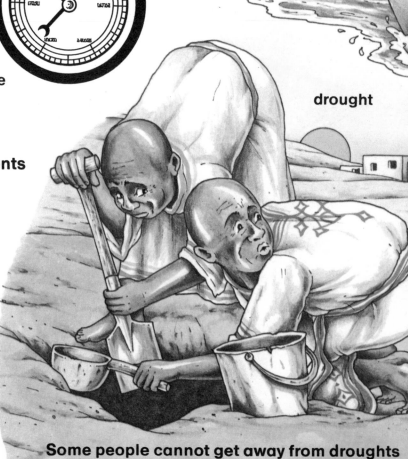

**Some people cannot get away from droughts
and floods. Bad weather causes suffering
in many parts of the world.**

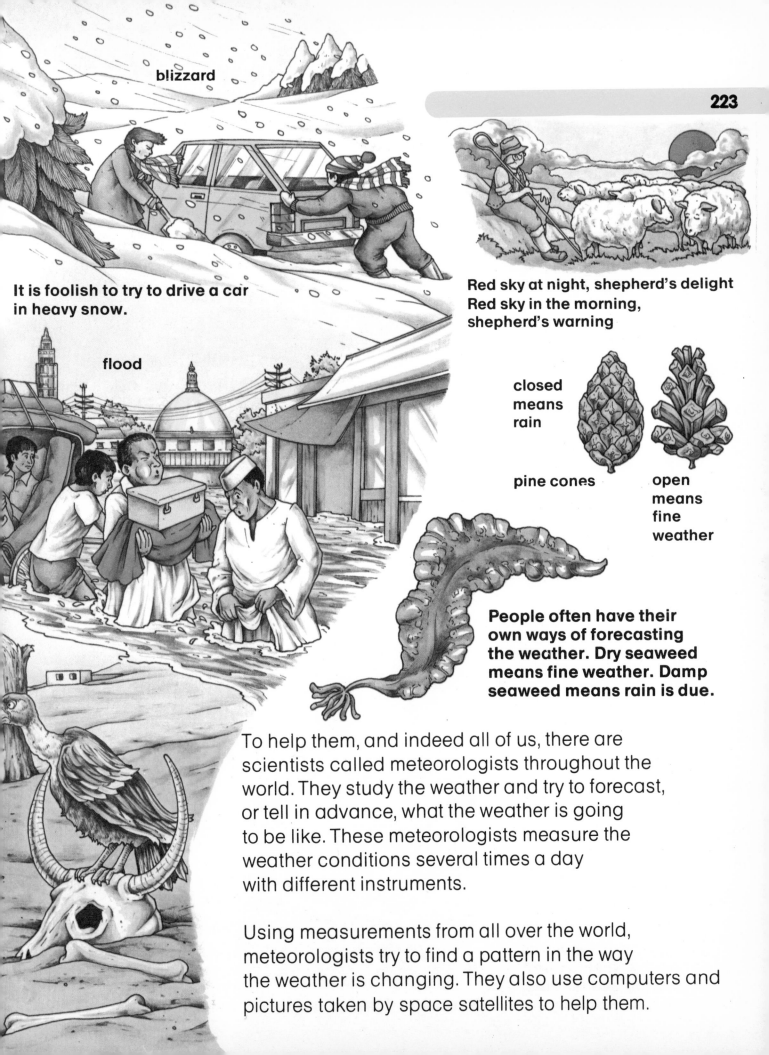

blizzard

It is foolish to try to drive a car in heavy snow.

flood

Red sky at night, shepherd's delight
Red sky in the morning, shepherd's warning

closed means rain

pine cones

open means fine weather

People often have their own ways of forecasting the weather. Dry seaweed means fine weather. Damp seaweed means rain is due.

To help them, and indeed all of us, there are scientists called meteorologists throughout the world. They study the weather and try to forecast, or tell in advance, what the weather is going to be like. These meteorologists measure the weather conditions several times a day with different instruments.

Using measurements from all over the world, meteorologists try to find a pattern in the way the weather is changing. They also use computers and pictures taken by space satellites to help them.

Wind power

Have you ever tried to hold an open umbrella in a strong wind? If you have, then you will know how much power the wind can have. Thousands of years ago, people found out how to use wind power to move their boats. They fixed a piece of cloth to a pole so that it could 'catch' the wind. They invented the sail.

With sailing boats, people could travel further and faster than they could when they paddled or rowed the boats. Sails were the main means of making ships move until steamships were built.

The wind can be useful for drying washing and scattering seeds. But it can cause damage.

Hurricane damage in Darwin, Australia.

These Egyptian boats are the same as those of 900 years ago. Their triangular sails help them to sail better than boats with square sails.

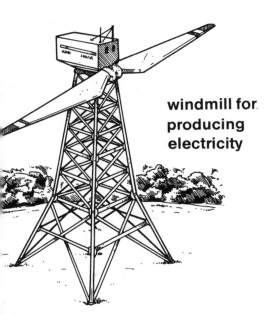

windmill for producing electricity

toy windmill

windmill for pumping water

windmill for grinding grain

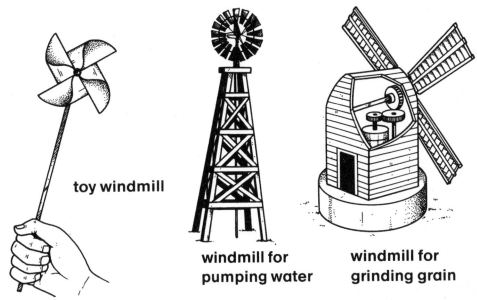

About a thousand years ago, people found a new use for wind power. This was to mill, or grind, grain into flour. They invented the windmill. It had large arms, or sails, that turned when the wind blew. As they spun round, they moved machinery that turned the millstones which ground the grain.

Windmills have many uses. The latest types have a propeller instead of sails.

Later, windmills were used to pump water for draining wet land. Today many farmers use windmills to pump water or to produce electricity.

Flying

On the wing

Have you ever wished you could fly like a bird? Many people have tried to fly. They fastened wings to their arms and began flapping them. But it did not work. People are not built to fly like birds. We are too heavy and our chest muscles are too weak. We must use our brains and invent flying machines to help us fly.

The first people to fly travelled in balloons. Balloons float in air rather like ships float in water.

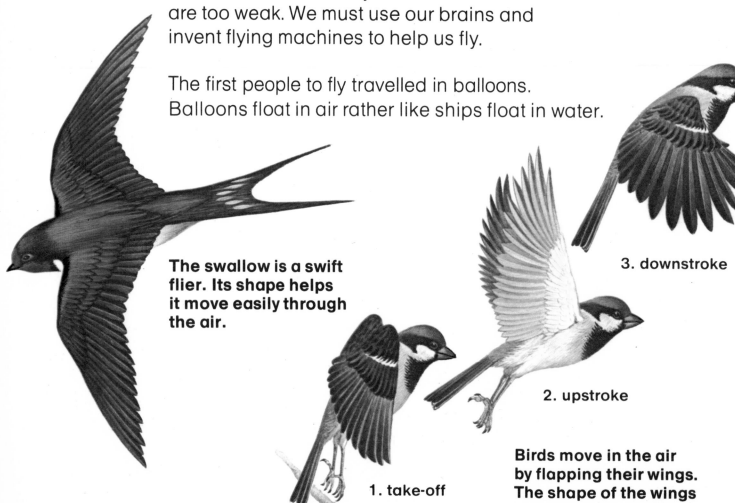

The swallow is a swift flier. Its shape helps it move easily through the air.

3. downstroke

2. upstroke

1. take-off

Birds move in the air by flapping their wings. The shape of the wings gives lift to keep the birds up in the air.

4. landing

The first balloons flew in 1783. They were, like these, filled with hot air. Some balloons used to be filled with hydrogen, like airships.

Airships are like balloons with engines. Airships have flown since 1900. The world's biggest airship was the Hindenburg, 247 metres long. It was destroyed in 1937 when it exploded on landing in the USA in a storm.

Building planes

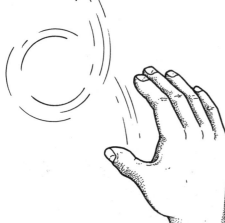

You can make your own paper glider. It flies because it has the right shape.

Balloons rise into the air because they are lighter than the air. How do birds stay up in the air when they are heavier than air? They stay up there because of the special shape of their wings. As they fly, it is their wings that give them lift.

Our most common flying machine, the aeroplane, or plane, is heavier than air. And it also must have wings of a special shape to stay up in the air. When the plane travels through the air, its wings develop lift which keeps it up.

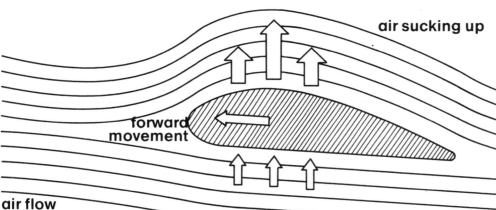

air sucking up

forward movement

air flow

air pushing up

Wings have a special shape, called an aerofoil. This shape provides the lift because of the way the air moves over it.

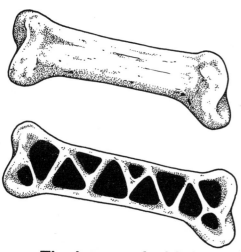

The bones of a bird are different from those of other animals. They are light but strong.

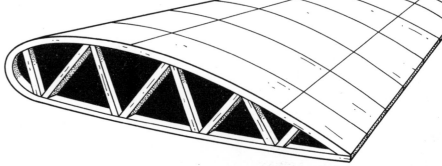

Plane wings are made in the same way as bird bones, to be light and strong.

forward movement

pressure

air escapes

The other main parts of a plane are the fuselage, tail and engines. The fuselage is the main body of the plane, which carries the passengers and cargo. The tail helps keep the plane steady, just as the flight feathers of a dart keep the dart travelling straight.

The engines provide the power to move the plane along. In the early days of flying all planes had engines rather like car engines and propellers to move them through the air. Most modern planes have jet engines.

A balloon travels by jet power when you let it go. Jet engines work in the same way. They are thrust forwards as gases shoot out backwards.

This was the world's first plane, which flew on December 17, 1903. It was flown by the Wright brothers in the USA.

This modern airliner is the Boeing 747 'jumbo' jet, which can carry over 400 passengers. It is 70 metres long. The Wright's plane was 6 metres long.

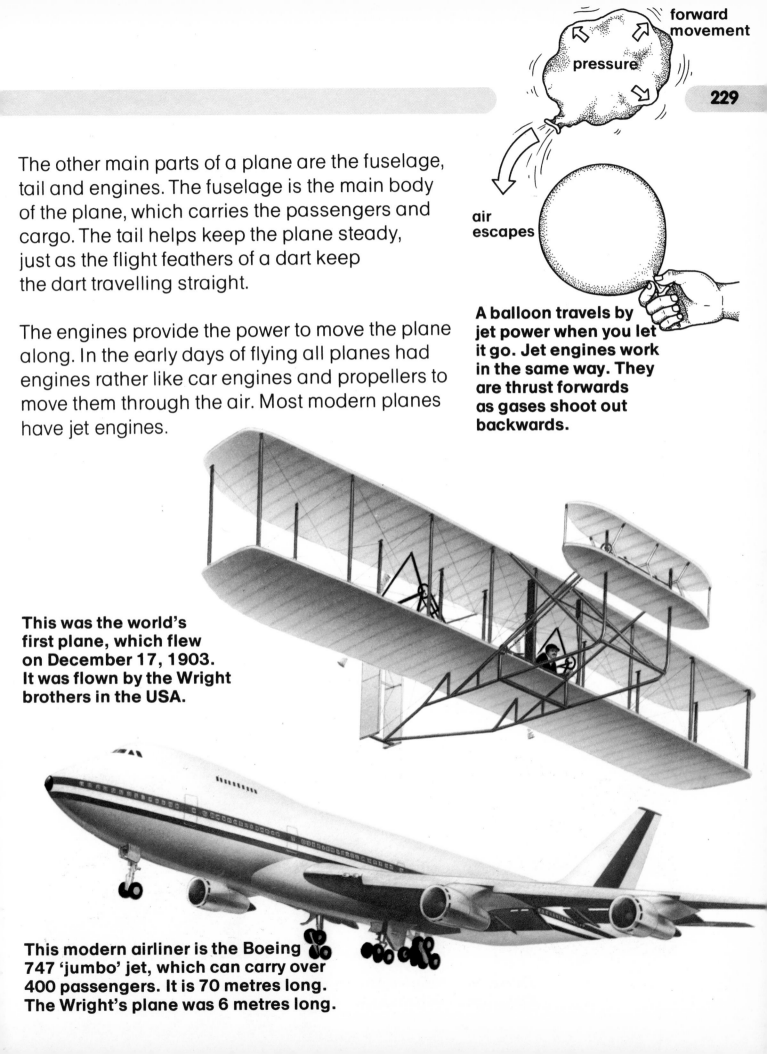

Travelling fast and far

Before the coming of the plane, travel over long distances was very slow indeed. It took ships about 6 days to cross the Atlantic Ocean between Britain and the USA. Today we can make the same journey by plane in only about 6 hours. Some planes, such as Concorde, take even less time. We can travel half way round the world in less than a day.

Air travel is not only fast, it is also cheaper than other ways of travelling long distances. More and more people are travelling by air, not just on business but also on holiday. We can visit distant countries and see how other people live.

There are planes from all over the world at this airport in Holland.

flying doctor service

air-sea rescue

crop spraying

herding cattle

Planes are not the only kind of aircraft, of course. Another one is the helicopter, which is a very different kind of flying machine. It does not have ordinary wings to lift it into the air. Long blades on top of its body produce lift when they turn round, or rotate. The helicopter is particularly useful because it can move straight up and down, sideways and backwards. It can also hover in one place in the air.

Planes and helicopters have all kinds of different uses. In some countries, doctors travel by plane to see patients.

Rocketing into space

Escaping from the Earth

It is very difficult to put something into space because the Earth has a strong pull, called gravity.

If you throw a ball into the air, it rises a certain distance and then falls back to the ground. Gravity pulls it back. But if you were superhuman and could throw the ball very fast indeed, it would go up and up and go into space.

On Earth, what goes up must come down! Gravity pulls everything back to the ground.

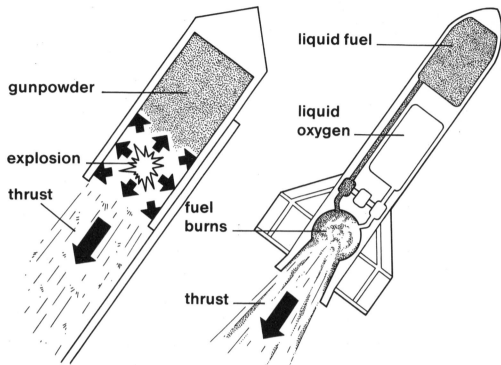

gunpowder

explosion

thrust

fuel burns

liquid fuel

liquid oxygen

thrust

A firework rocket burns solid fuel to make hot gases. As the gases rush backwards, the rocket is pushed forwards.

Space rockets usually work on liquid fuel. It is mixed with liquid oxygen and burns inside the rocket.

The American space shuttle is launched from Earth by powerful rockets. Only the winged part, the orbiter, goes into space. The rest falls back to Earth.

The only way to get anything into space is by using the power of a rocket engine. A rocket is also the only engine that can work in space where there is no air. All other engines have to use oxygen from the air to be able to burn their fuel. Rockets work because they carry their own supply of oxygen.

In 1957, for the first time, an object from Earth escaped into space. It was launched by the Russians and called Sputnik 1. Since then thousands of spacecraft have been launched. Some have even travelled to distant planets.

Satellites and probes

Objects launched into space are called spacecraft. Most spacecraft travel in a circular path, or orbit, that takes them round and round the Earth.

These craft, called satellites, may orbit round the Earth for years. There are many kinds of satellites. Astronomy satellites gather information about the stars and space. Weather satellites take pictures of cloud patterns over the Earth, which meteorologists find very useful. Earth-survey satellites collect information about the Earth's surface.

Television signals from Paris travel to a French satellite ground station. A huge dish aerial beams them up to a communications satellite, 36,000 kilometres above the Atlantic Ocean.

Communications satellites pass on radio signals from country to country. These signals carry telephone conversations and television programmes. Communications satellites are placed very high up so that they can keep in touch with a large part of the Earth's surface.

Other spacecraft leave the Earth and travel to the Moon and the planets. They are called probes and can send us information about space. Satellites and probes do not need to carry people to work them. They are robots.

The satellite receives the signals and makes them stronger. It then beams them towards the USA.

In the USA another ground station aerial receives the signals and passes them to a New York transmitter. This broadcasts the French television programme to people in the city. At the same time, American programmes can be passed back to France.

Living in space

Sometimes people travel into space. They are called astronauts or cosmonauts. They go into space to carry out experiments or to launch satellites. They fly in large spacecraft that have their own supplies of air, food and water.

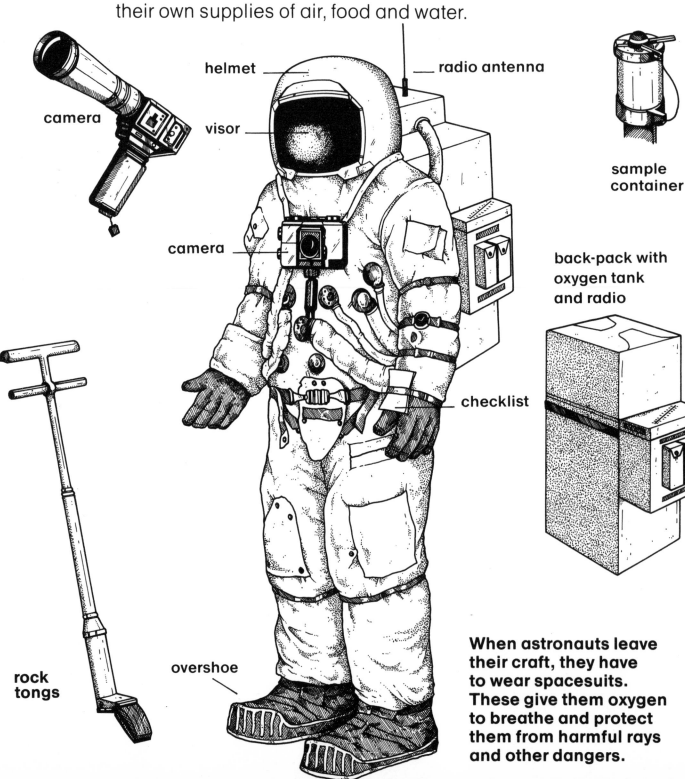

camera

helmet

visor

camera

radio antenna

sample container

back-pack with oxygen tank and radio

checklist

rock tongs

overshoe

When astronauts leave their craft, they have to wear spacesuits. These give them oxygen to breathe and protect them from harmful rays and other dangers.

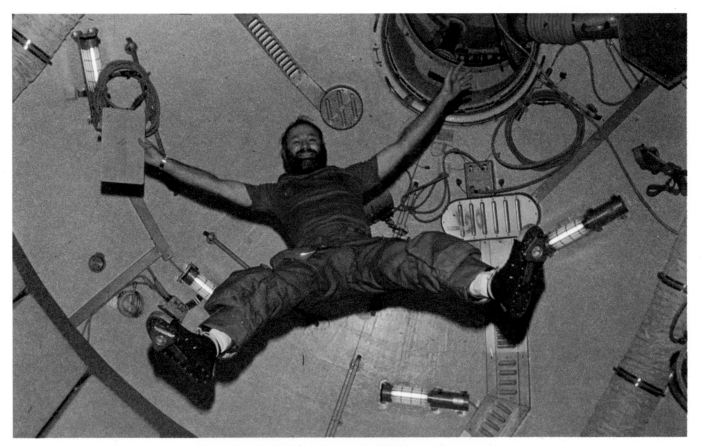

**When people are weightless in space,
they can float inside their spacecraft.
This astronaut was photographed
inside Skylab.**

If you travelled into space, you would find
life there very different from life on Earth. The
strangest thing that happens is that you have no weight.

Everything in space is weightless. Nothing falls
when you let go of it. It just remains floating
in mid-air. You cannot drink liquid from a glass,
because there is no gravity to make the liquid
pour out. You cannot walk properly because
there is no gravity to keep your feet on the floor.
You have to move by pushing or pulling yourself along.

In this weightless state, your muscles would get
lazy and so you would have to be careful to take
regular exercise to keep fit.

The great adventure

People have already travelled in spacecraft to the Moon and landed there. One day people might return to the Moon and set up permanent bases there. Between the Earth and the Moon there could be huge space colonies, where thousands of people would live. There, they might make things of great use to us, such as new medicines, which cannot now be made on Earth.

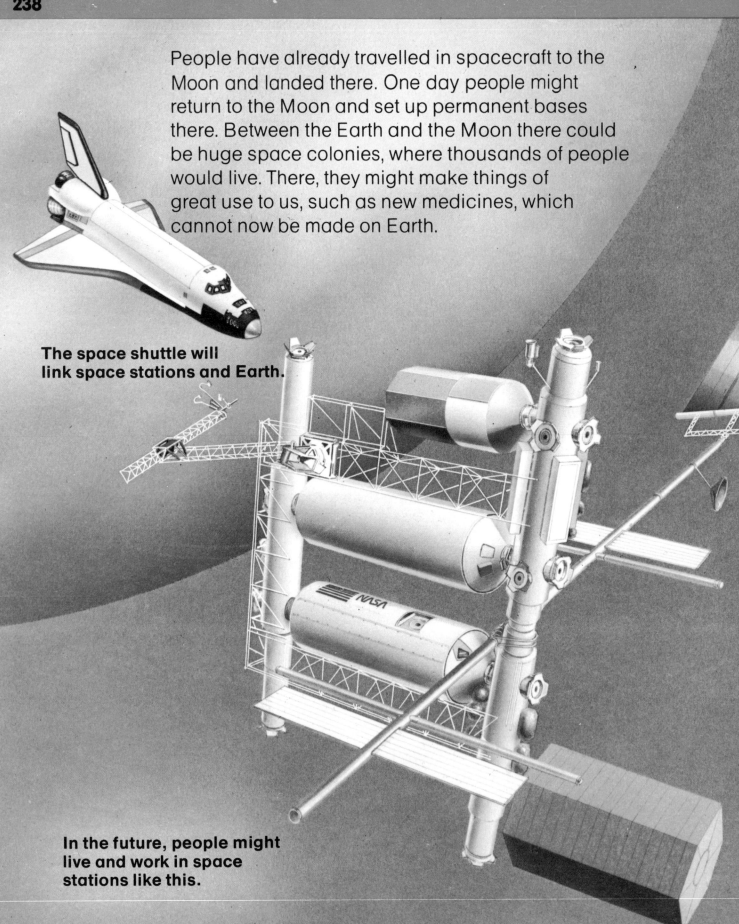

The space shuttle will link space stations and Earth.

In the future, people might live and work in space stations like this.

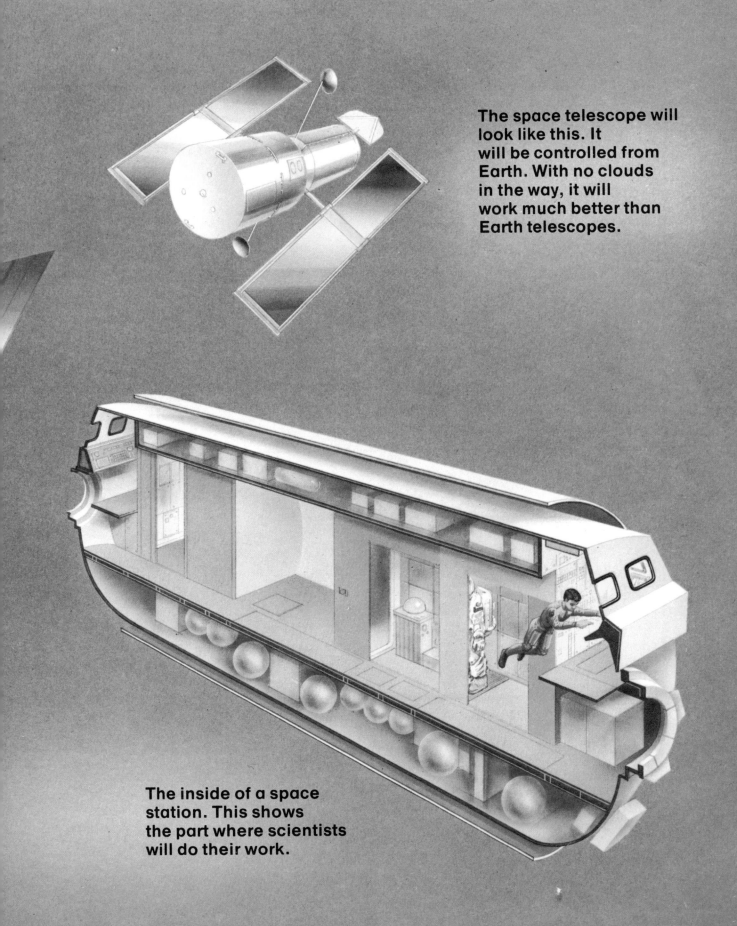

The space telescope will look like this. It will be controlled from Earth. With no clouds in the way, it will work much better than Earth telescopes.

The inside of a space station. This shows the part where scientists will do their work.

10

My First Atlas

Michael Weller

What is a map?

Imagine you are going on a trip around the world.
An aeroplane is ready to take you to each of
the landing places in each continent.

The maps in your atlas will help you to find
your way around. Pictures will give you some ideas
about what it is like to live in different places
in the world.

▲ This jumbo jet is too
big to draw full size. But
you can work out its size
as in real life by reading
the scale line on a map
or plan.

Here is a plan of the Jumbo
jet seen from above. The
scale line tells you that
1 cm on the plan is the
same as 8 metres on the
ground. How long is the
aeroplane on the plan in
centimetres? How long is
the aeroplane on the
ground in metres? ▶

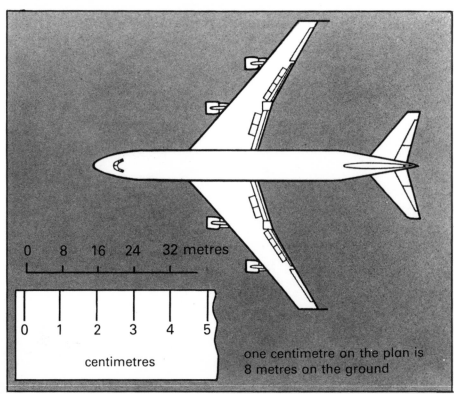

0   8   16   24   32 metres

0   1   2   3   4   5
centimetres

one centimetre on the plan is
8 metres on the ground

The key tells you what
the map shows. ▼

 Runway

 Concrete

Grass

Aeroplane

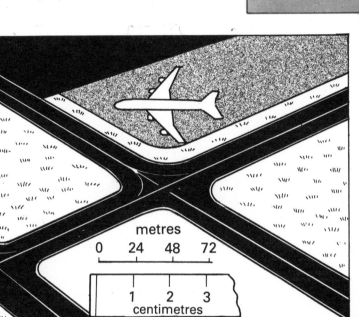

metres

0   24   48   72

1   2   3

centimetres

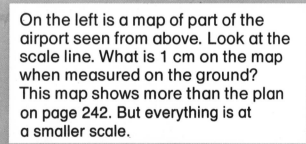

On the left is a map of part of the
airport seen from above. Look at the
scale line. What is 1 cm on the map
when measured on the ground?
This map shows more than the plan
on page 242. But everything is at
a smaller scale.

Try pacing the real size
of the aeroplane
in the playground.

Maps and globes

When you take off in the aeroplane you can look back
to see the ground like a map. As you climb higher,
you will see more of the landscape. But it will be
difficult to see small things like a house.

Everything will be at a small scale.
Can you see the river in the photograph?
What else can you see?

▲ Imagine you are aboard
the jumbo jet, looking
out of the window.
Everything looks very
small. But you can see the
river leading to the sea.

This map shows the river
that you can see in the
photograph. What else
does the map show? What
is the scale of the map?
Try to use the scale to
measure how long
the river is. ▶

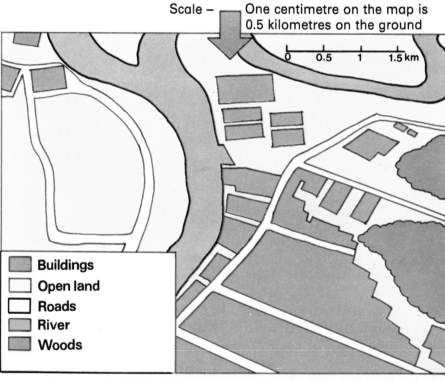

Scale – One centimetre on the map is
0.5 kilometres on the ground

0   0.5   1   1.5 km

Buildings
Open land
Roads
River
Woods

People in spacecraft go high enough to see the whole of our planet Earth. They can take photographs like the one on the front of this atlas.
You can look at a model of planet Earth if you have a globe. The picture shows part of a globe.
You can see the curve of the planet. Can you see Europe on it? If you have a globe, look for Europe on it.

This child has a globe. She is trying to make a map of the Earth on a sheet of paper. Try to do this. Why is it difficult to make a flat map of the whole Earth?

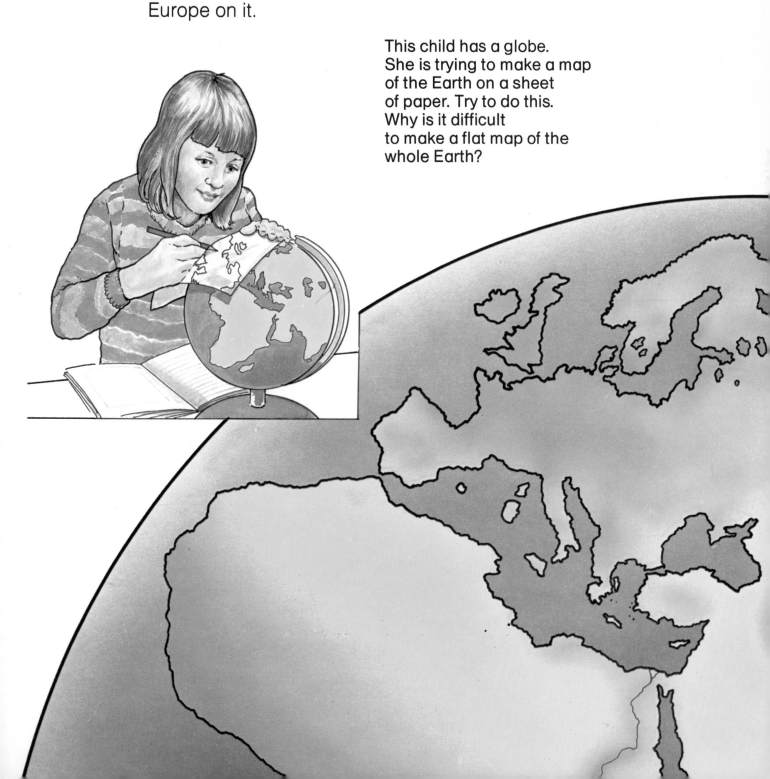

Going places

Map-makers have made this map to show you
the whole world. We have put on the routes that
you will fly on your journey. You can see
the different continents and oceans that
you will cross. Look closely at their names.
The map shows your landing place in each
continent. Which landing place is furthest
from London?

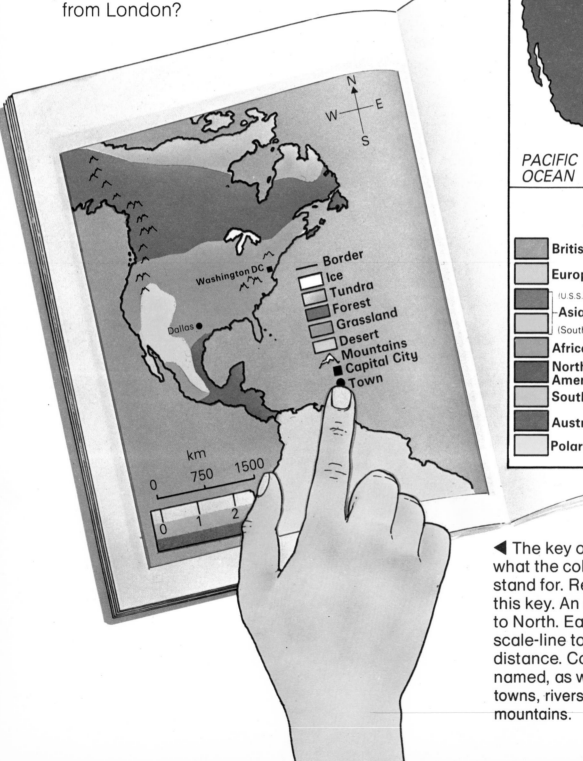

Border
Ice
Tundra
Forest
Grassland
Desert
Mountains
Capital City
Town

Washington DC

Dallas

km
0   750   1500

0   1   2

New Yo

9½ ho

CENTRAL
AMERICA

PACIFIC
OCEAN

British Isles

Europe

(U.S.S.R. in Asia)

Asia

(South of the U.S.S.R.)

Africa

North and Central
America

South America

Australasia

Polar regions

◀ The key on this map shows
what the colours and symbols
stand for. Remember to look at
this key. An arrow points
to North. Each map has a
scale-line to measure
distance. Countries are
named, as well as some
towns, rivers and
mountains.

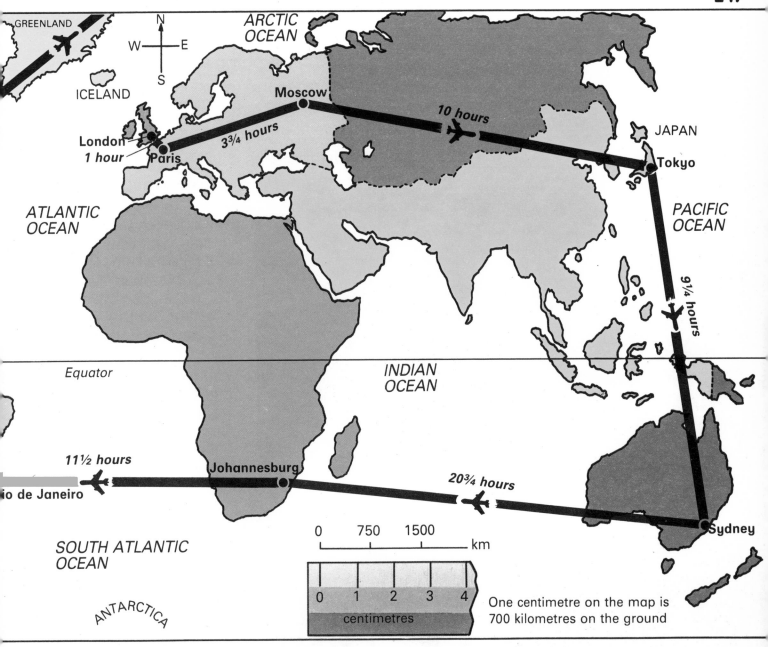

GREENLAND

ARCTIC OCEAN

ICELAND

N
W — E
S

Moscow

London
1 hour
Paris

3¾ hours

10 hours

JAPAN

Tokyo

PACIFIC OCEAN

ATLANTIC OCEAN

9¼ hours

Equator

INDIAN OCEAN

11½ hours

Johannesburg

20¾ hours

Rio de Janeiro

Sydney

SOUTH ATLANTIC OCEAN

ANTARCTICA

0   750   1500
|—————————| km

0   1   2   3   4
centimetres

One centimetre on the map is
700 kilometres on the ground

▲ This map helps you to work out how far apart places are and how long your trip will take by air.

It is not easy to make the globe into a flat map, as you may have found out. If you peeled the skin off a globe you would have to cut it to make it lie flat.

Some of your neighbours on the aeroplane live in the British Isles. Some are travelling to work or to a holiday, or to see relatives. The map shows the British Isles but it cannot show people's homes on this scale. Pictures can show you the homes and communities people live in.

◀ All over the world people live in small places. Not all small places look like Shaftesbury here. Try to find it on the map. It is near Southampton in the south of England.

You will find cities like this in many parts of the world. Some of the people living and working in these buildings come from other parts of the world. ▼

▲ The people who live here in Newcastle probably work in town but can enjoy the countryside as well. Use the map to see where it is.

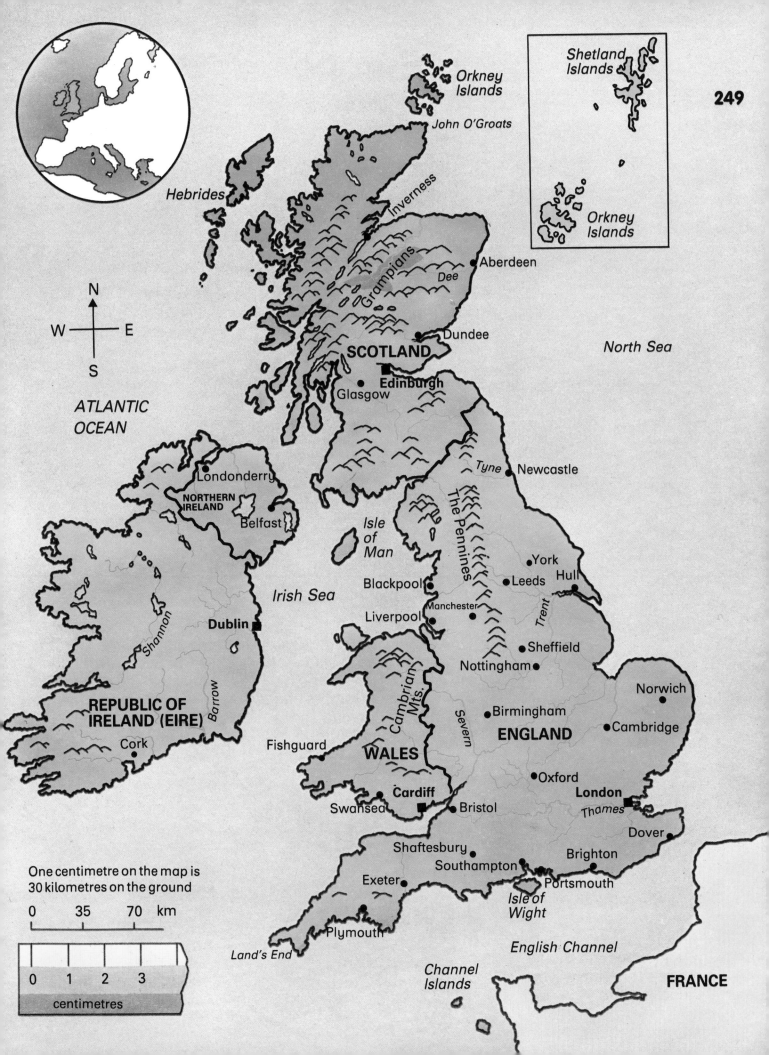

Orkney Islands

John O'Groats

Shetland Islands

Orkney Islands

Hebrides

Inverness

Grampians

Dee

Aberdeen

North Sea

Dundee

SCOTLAND

Edinburgh

Glasgow

ATLANTIC OCEAN

N
W E
S

Londonderry

NORTHERN IRELAND

Belfast

Tyne

Newcastle

Isle of Man

The Pennines

York

Hull

Blackpool

Leeds

Shannon

Dublin

Irish Sea

Manchester

Liverpool

Trent

Sheffield

Nottingham

REPUBLIC OF IRELAND (EIRE)

Barrow

Cambrian Mts.

Severn

Birmingham

Norwich

ENGLAND

Cambridge

Cork

WALES

Fishguard

Oxford

London

Cardiff

Swansea

Bristol

Thames

Dover

Shaftesbury

Brighton

Southampton

Portsmouth

Exeter

Isle of Wight

Plymouth

Land's End

Channel Islands

English Channel

FRANCE

One centimetre on the map is 30 kilometres on the ground

0   35   70   km

0   1   2   3

centimetres

Our first stop is at Paris airport near the capital city of France. Can you count how many countries there are in Europe? A border is the line where one country touches another.
in each country people work in many different jobs, as in England. Sometimes, people have to travel to another country to find work.

One of our passengers works in a warehouse in Denmark. He drives a fork-lift truck. The warehouse stores cheese which is then sold to shops in other parts of Europe. ▼

▲ Europe has some farmers like this. This one lives in Spain. What can you see in the picture? Look for Spain on the map. What does the map tell you about the area?

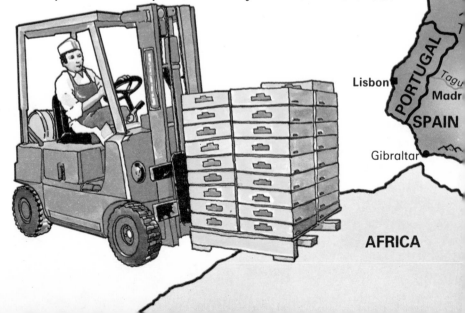

▲ Here in Italy, ships are made at Ancona. Name the sea this ship will be launched into.

PORTUGAL

Lisbon

Tagu

Madr

SPAIN

Gibraltar

AFRICA

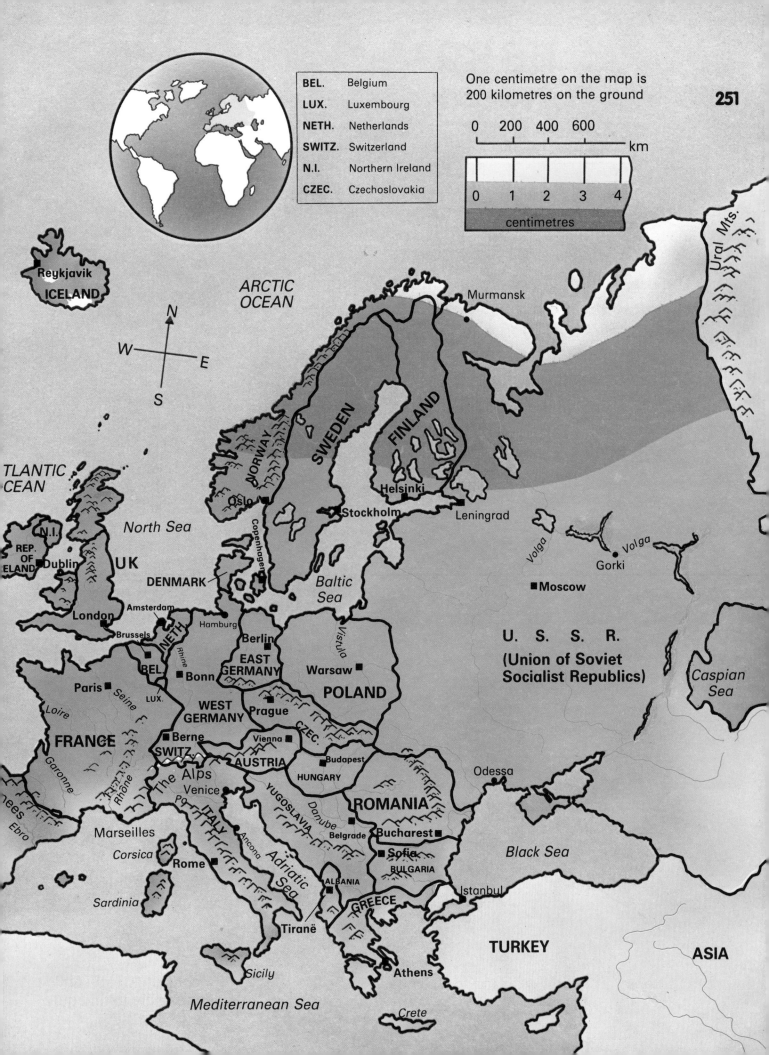

BEL. Belgium
LUX. Luxembourg
NETH. Netherlands
SWITZ. Switzerland
N.I. Northern Ireland
CZEC. Czechoslovakia

One centimetre on the map is
200 kilometres on the ground

0   200   400   600
km

0   1   2   3   4
centimetres

Reykjavik
ICELAND

ARCTIC
OCEAN

Murmansk

Ural Mts.

N
W   E
S

TLANTIC
CEAN

NORWAY

SWEDEN

FINLAND

Helsinki

Oslo

Stockholm

Leningrad

North Sea

Copenhagen

Baltic
Sea

Volga

Volga

Gorki

Moscow

N.I.

REP.
OF
ELAND

Dublin

UK

London

Amsterdam

NETH.

Hamburg

DENMARK

Berlin

EAST
GERMANY

Vistula

Warsaw

POLAND

U. S. S. R.
(Union of Soviet
Socialist Republics)

Caspian
Sea

Brussels

BEL.

Rhine

Paris

LUX.

Seine

WEST
GERMANY

Prague

CZEC.

Loire

Bonn

FRANCE

Berne

SWITZ.

Vienna

AUSTRIA

Budapest

HUNGARY

Odessa

Garonne

Rhone

The Alps

Venice

YUGOSLAVIA

Danube

ROMANIA

Belgrade

Bucharest

nees

Ebro

Marseilles

Corsica

ITALY

Ancona

Adriatic
Sea

Sofia

BULGARIA

Black Sea

Rome

ALBANIA

Sardinia

Tiranë

GREECE

Istanbul

Sicily

Athens

TURKEY

ASIA

Mediterranean Sea

Crete

Your next stop is Moscow, the capital of the U.S.S.R. The U.S.S.R. is the biggest country in the world. People have to travel long distances and so transport is very important.

The U.S.S.R. stretches across Europe and Asia. Most people speak Russian but some speak other languages. Most people live in the European part of the country, which is the part called Russia. The U.S.S.R. has many ships, aeroplanes, cars and lorries. It has space rockets like the Americans.

POLAND

Leningrad

Moscow

Kiev

Kharkov

Odessa

Don

Black Sea

TURKEY

IRAN

◀ The Trans-Siberian railway runs from the Ural Mountains to Vladivostok. How far is this? Use the scale to find out.

ARCTIC
OCEAN

Murmansk

Arkhangelsk

Bering
Sea

Lena

UNION OF SOVIET SOCIALIST REPUBLICS

Yienisei

Sea of
Okhotsk

Ural Mts.

Sverdlovsk

Omsk

Novosibirsk

Ob

Irkutsk

Amur

CHINA

Vladivostock

Ural

MONGOLIA

JAPAN

Tashkent

Samarkand

N
W   E
S

0   400   800   1200
km

0   1   2   3   4
centimetres

PACIFIC
OCEAN

One centimetre on the map is
400 kilometres on the ground

▲ The Moscow metro is a fast
and cheap way of moving people
around. It is usually crowded
while the roads are free of traffic.

▲ Huge forests stretch across the northlands.
Giant lorries haul out the timber. Try to
find some pictures of transport in the U.S.S.R.

It takes eight days by train from Moscow to Vladivostock. By air you could reach Tokyo, capital of Japan, in less than ten hours.

Asia is the largest continent in the world. More than half of the world's people live in Asia. All the great religions of the world began there. Judaism, Christianity and Islam began in Asia. Buddhism and Hinduism started in India. All these religions have spread across the world. Do any of your friends practise one of these religions?

I	Israel
N.	Nepal
Q	Quatar
J.	Jordan
Y	Yemen
K	Kuwait
B	Bhutan
L	Lebanon
BA.	Bahrain
BD	Bangladesh
U.A.E.	United Arab Emirates

Hindus believe in one god, Brahman, but they pray to the many gods who represent him. Here, some Hindus are washing themselves in the waters of a holy river. What rivers are shown on the map of India? ▼

▲ Muhammed, the prophet of Islam, was born in Mecca. Where is this holy city on the map? Here Muslims perform their daily worship. What country is Mecca in?

This family is paying respect to a statue of Buddha. Buddhists follow sets of rules which shape their life. Notice the way they join hands as a sign of respect. ▶

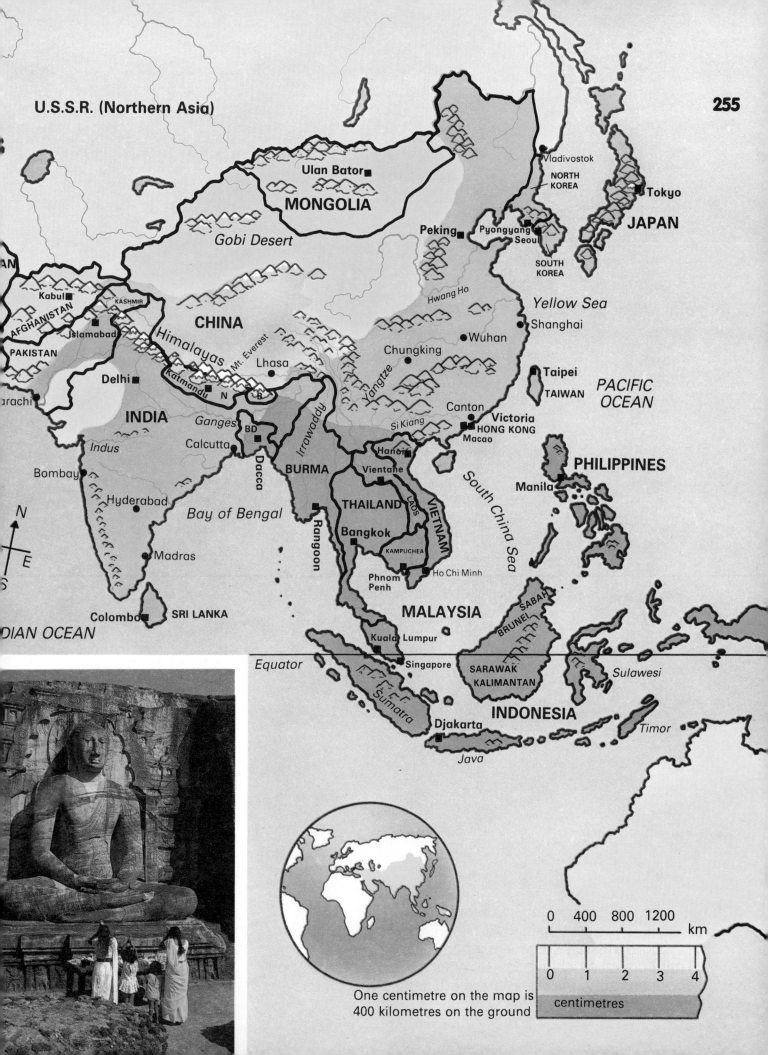

Ulan Bator

MONGOLIA

Gobi Desert

Vladivostok

NORTH KOREA

Tokyo

Peking

Pyongyang
Seoul

JAPAN

Kabul

KASHMIR

AFGHANISTAN

Islamabad

PAKISTAN

CHINA

SOUTH KOREA

Yellow Sea

Hwang Ho

Shanghai

Delhi

Himalayas

Mt. Everest

Lhasa

Katmandu

N

Wuhan

Chungking

Yangtze

arachi

INDIA

Ganges

BD

Calcutta

Dacca

Indus

Bombay

Hyderabad

Irrawaddy

BURMA

Si Kiang

Canton

Taipei

TAIWAN

PACIFIC OCEAN

Victoria
HONG KONG
Macao

Hanoi

Vientane

Madras

Bay of Bengal

Rangoon

THAILAND

Bangkok

LAOS

VIETNAM

South China Sea

PHILIPPINES

Manila

N

E

S

Colombo

SRI LANKA

KAMPUCHEA

Ho Chi Minh

Phnom
Penh

DIAN OCEAN

MALAYSIA

SABAH

BRUNEI

Kuala Lumpur

Equator

Singapore

SARAWAK
KALIMANTAN

Sulawesi

Sumatra

INDONESIA

Djakarta

Timor

Java

0	400	800	1200

km

0	1	2	3	4

centimetres

One centimetre on the map is
400 kilometres on the ground

Australasia
Resources

Between Japan and Australia is the South Pacific Ocean. This ocean covers nearly half the surface of the Earth. It contains thousands of islands. The largest, Australia, is also called a continent.

Fish and crops are harvested on islands like Sulawesi. Sheep, cattle and wheat are important resources in Australia and New Zealand. These products are sent to the rest of the world. Minerals are also sold to other countries.

Sheep are a main resource in New Zealand. What other resources does the country have? Look on food labels in your larder at home. Do any come from New Zealand?

This shows coal mining in Yallourn, Victoria, Australia. Australia has other minerals, like iron, gold and uranium. What are these resources used for?
There are also rich farmlands. What does the map tell you about central Australia? Where are most of the cities?

CHINA

ASIA

PHILIPPINES

Sulawesi

PAPUA
GU

INDONESIA

Timor Sea — Darwin

NORTHERN TERRITORY

Great Sandy Desert

AUSTRALIA

Alice Springs ●

WESTERN AUSTRALIA

Great Victoria Desert

SOUTH AUSTRALIA

Kalgoorlie ●

Perth ●

Adelaid

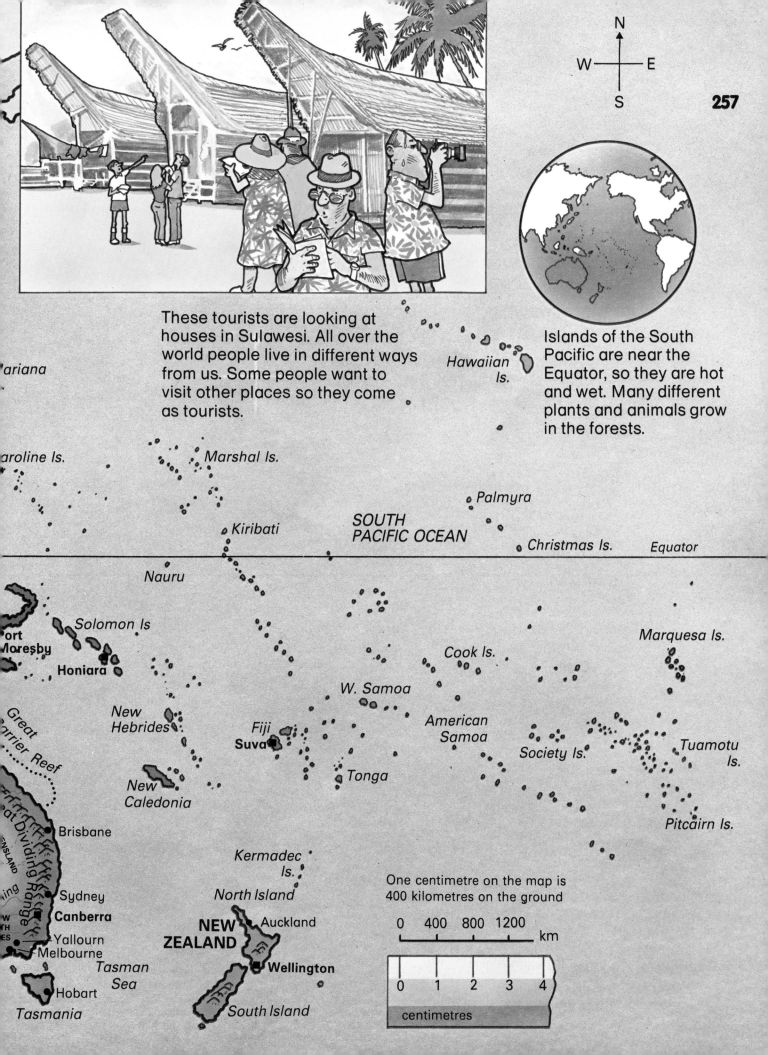

These tourists are looking at houses in Sulawesi. All over the world people live in different ways from us. Some people want to visit other places so they come as tourists.

Islands of the South Pacific are near the Equator, so they are hot and wet. Many different plants and animals grow in the forests.

Mariana

Hawaiian Is.

aroline Is.

Marshal Is.

Palmyra

Kiribati

SOUTH PACIFIC OCEAN

Christmas Is.

Equator

Nauru

Solomon Is

Marquesa Is.

ort Moresby

Cook Is.

Honiara

W. Samoa

New Hebrides

American Samoa

Fiji

Society Is.

Tuamotu Is.

Suva

Tonga

New Caledonia

Pitcairn Is.

Great Barrier Reef

Brisbane

Kermadec Is.

One centimetre on the map is 400 kilometres on the ground

Sydney

North Island

Canberra

Auckland

0   400   800   1200

NEW ZEALAND

Yallourn

km

Melbourne

Tasman Sea

Wellington

0   1   2   3   4

Hobart

South Island

centimetres

Tasmania

Africa
Landscapes

From Sydney you fly across Australia to Perth. To reach Africa you then cross the Indian ocean to Johannesburg in South Africa.

Africa has many different landscapes. Near the equator are large forests. Much of the continent is covered in tropical grasslands. Most of the farms are found here. In the north and in the south there are deserts. In east Africa you can find snow-capped mountains. The map shows that there are many great rivers and lakes.

▲ Zebra and impalas are found in the grasslands. In National parks, they can roam freely. What do you think about keeping animals in zoos?

Desert landscape is mainly sand and rock. Living there is difficult. Plants that can store water can live there. Do you know any? How do you think people live in hot deserts? ▶

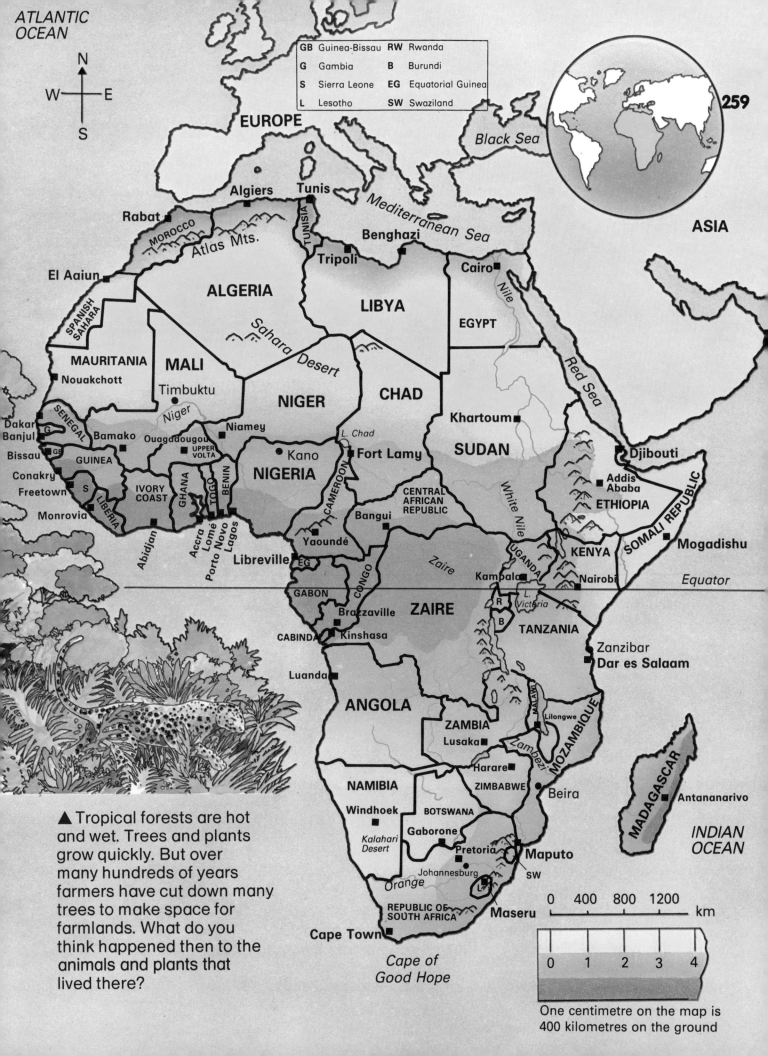

ATLANTIC
OCEAN

N
W E
S

259

EUROPE

GB	Guinea-Bissau	RW	Rwanda
G	Gambia	B	Burundi
S	Sierra Leone	EG	Equatorial Guinea
L	Lesotho	SW	Swaziland

Black Sea

Mediterranean Sea

ASIA

Algiers Tunis

Rabat MOROCCO TUNISIA Benghazi

Atlas Mts. Tripoli Cairo

El Aaiun

SPANISH SAHARA **ALGERIA** **LIBYA** **EGYPT** Nile

Sahara Desert

MAURITANIA **MALI** **NIGER** **CHAD** Red Sea

Nouakchott Timbuktu Khartoum Djibouti

Niger Niamey L. Chad **SUDAN** Addis Ababa

Dakar SENEGAL Bamako Ouagadougou Kano Fort Lamy **ETHIOPIA** SOMALI REPUBLIC

Banjul G UPPER VOLTA **NIGERIA** CAMEROON White Nile

Bissau GB GUINEA BENIN CENTRAL AFRICAN REPUBLIC

Conakry S IVORY COAST GHANA TOGO Bangui KENYA Mogadishu

Freetown LIBERIA

Monrovia Accra Lomé Lagos Yaoundé Zaire UGANDA Nairobi *Equator*

Abidjan Porto Novo Libreville EG Kampala

CONGO GABON L. Victoria

Brazzaville **ZAIRE** R

CABINDA Kinshasa B **TANZANIA**

Luanda Zanzibar Dar es Salaam

ANGOLA MALAWI

ZAMBIA Lilongwe MOZAMBIQUE

Lusaka

Harare

NAMIBIA ZIMBABWE Beira

Windhoek BOTSWANA Antananarivo

Kalahari Desert Gaborone MADAGASCAR

Pretoria Maputo INDIAN OCEAN

Johannesburg SW

Orange L

REPUBLIC OF SOUTH AFRICA Maseru

Cape Town

Cape of Good Hope

▲ Tropical forests are hot
and wet. Trees and plants
grow quickly. But over
many hundreds of years
farmers have cut down many
trees to make space for
farmlands. What do you
think happened then to the
animals and plants that
lived there?

0 400 800 1200 km

0 1 2 3 4

One centimetre on the map is
400 kilometres on the ground

South America
Culture

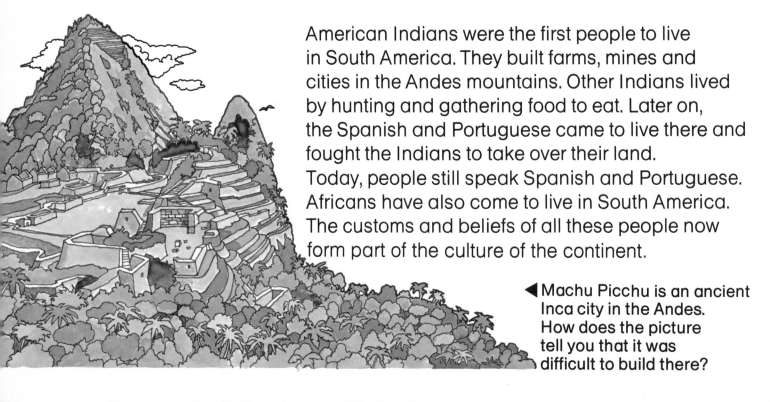

American Indians were the first people to live in South America. They built farms, mines and cities in the Andes mountains. Other Indians lived by hunting and gathering food to eat. Later on, the Spanish and Portuguese came to live there and fought the Indians to take over their land.

Today, people still speak Spanish and Portuguese. Africans have also come to live in South America. The customs and beliefs of all these people now form part of the culture of the continent.

◄ Machu Picchu is an ancient Inca city in the Andes. How does the picture tell you that it was difficult to build there?

▲ Brasilia's cathedral is one of the modern buildings in this new city. Brasilia is the new capital of Brazil. Find out why it was built inland.

Rio de Janeiro is well-known for its carnival. What do you notice about the people's clothes? How are they celebrating? ▶

F.G. French Guinea
S.   Surinam
E   Ecuador

Gulf of Mexico

West Indies

ATLANTIC
OCEAN

Caribbean Sea

Trinidad
Port of Spain

Panama
Canal

N
W   E
S

Caracas

VENEZUELA

Orinoco

Georgetown
Paramaribo
Cayenne

GUYANA

S

F.G.

Bogotá

COLOMBIA

Equator

Quito

E

Amazon

Belém

Fortaleza

PACIFIC
OCEAN

Manaus

PERU

Amazon

BRAZIL

São Francisco

Andes

Salvador

Lima

Lake
Titacaca

BOLIVIA

La Paz

Brazilia

Brazilian Highlands

Arequipa

Sucre

PARAGUAY

Iguacu
Falls

Rio de Janeiro

São
Paulo

CHILE

Ascunción

Paraná

ARGENTINA

URUGUAY

Santiago

Concepción

Andes

Buenos
Aires

Montevideo

Falkland
Islands

One centimetre on the map is
400 kilometres on the ground

0   400   800 1200
|----|----|----|----| km

Punta Arenas

Cape Horn

0   1   2   3   4

North and Central America

Weather

Flying from Rio in South America to New York in the U.S.A., you cross the equator. You fly over Central America and the West Indies.

The climate and weather change very much over this country. There are forests, deserts, grasslands and tundra lands. Indian, Eskimo, European and African people have all come to live there. The weather can make life very difficult sometimes. For example, there is burning sun in the desert in the south-west and it is icy cold in the north.

◄ Sometimes, there are very strong winds or tornadoes in the centre of the U.S.A. They make dust-storms and can blow over people's homes.

Near the Gulf of Mexico it is warm and wet. Heavy rain can make rivers like the Mississippi flood. ▶

ASIA

ARCTIC
OCEAN

Bering Strait

GREENLAND

Baffin Bay

Baffin Island

ALASKA
U.S.A.
Anchorage

Mackenzie

*Great
Bear Lake*

Great Slave Lake

Hudson Bay

Churchill

Newfoundland

St. John's

PACIFIC
OCEAN

Rocky

Edmonton

Calgary

Winnipeg

CANADA

Quebec

Montreal
Ottawa

Halifax

ATLANTIC
OCEAN

Vancouver

Seattle

Mountains

*L.
Superior*

Toronto

*L.
Huron*

Boston

New York

Washington DC

San
Francisco

Salt Lake
City

Minneapolis

U.S.A.

St. Louis

Missouri

Chicago

L. Michigan

Detroit

Appalachian Mts.

Los Angeles

Colorado

Denver

Mississippi

El Paso

Rio Grande

Dallas
Houston

Birmingham

MEXICO

Mexico
City

New
Orleans

Miami

Gulf of Mexico

West Indies

DOMINICAN
REP.

Havana

CUBA

HAITI

PUERTO
RICO

Santo
Domingo

Kingston

Port au
Prince

BELIZE

JAMAICA

Caribbean Sea

HONDURAS

NICARAGUA
*Panama
Canal*

GUATEMALA

EL SALVADOR

COSTA RICA

PANAMA

SOUTH AMERICA

▲ Few people live in the
tundra lands of Canada.
Eskimoes or Inuit first
lived there but their way
of life has changed.
Skidoos now replace
sledges pulled by dogs.

0   400   800   1200
                          km

0   1   2   3   4
centimetres

One centimetre on the map is
400 kilometres on the ground

Equator

PACIFIC OCEAN

CANADA

There is ice and snow round both Poles. The North Pole is at the centre of an ocean. The South Pole is the centre of a continent. Find out from the map the names of the ocean and the continent.

Very few people live there. Aircraft flying from Europe to countries around the Pacific Ocean cross the Arctic Ocean. Nuclear submarines cruise below the ice-covered sea. Early explorers travelled by dog sledge. Today, explorers use special tractors and aircraft. Explorers have to protect themselves against the cold.

ATLANTIC OCEAN

THE ARCTIC

▲ This ice-breaker from the U.S.S.R. helps to keep the coast of the U.S.S.R. free from ice in summer. The job is dangerous because of icebergs floating in the sea.

This man is a scientist working in Antarctica. He is using a balloon to study weather. In the middle of winter it is dark all day. In the middle of summer there are 24 hours of daylight. ▶

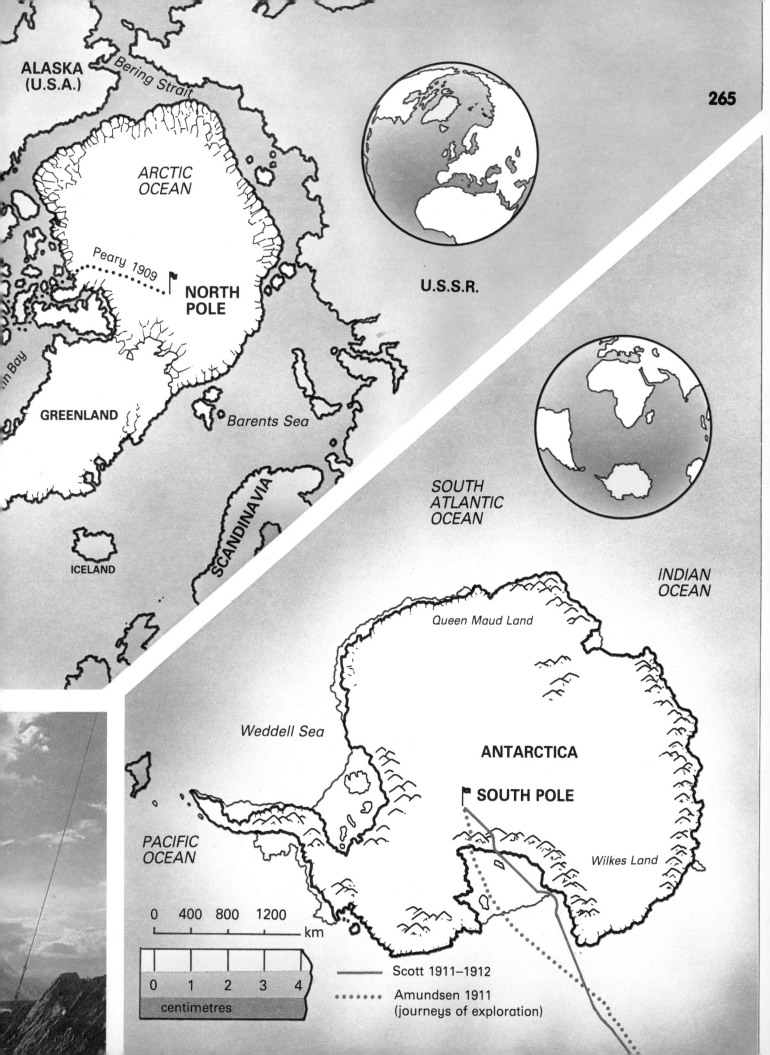

ALASKA
(U.S.A.)

Bering Strait

ARCTIC
OCEAN

Peary 1909

NORTH
POLE

GREENLAND

Barents Sea

ICELAND

SCANDINAVIA

U.S.S.R.

SOUTH
ATLANTIC
OCEAN

INDIAN
OCEAN

Queen Maud Land

Weddell Sea

ANTARCTICA

SOUTH POLE

Wilkes Land

PACIFIC
OCEAN

0   400   800   1200
                    km

0   1   2   3   4
centimetres

——— Scott 1911–1912

•••••• Amundsen 1911
(journeys of exploration)

INDEX

Acknowledgements

Illustrations
Peter Bailey/Linda Rogers Associates: 40-41, 46-47, 63, 73, 74-75, 119, 130.
Ann Baum/Linda Rogers Associates: 174-175, 178-179.
Peter Dennis/Linda Rogers Associates: 34-35, 38-39, 42-43, 58, 62, 64-65, 68, 72, 80, 82, 164-165, 166-167, 168, 170-171, 172-173, 180, 183, 187.
David Eaton: 222, 225, 228-229, 232-233, 236.
David Mostyn/Linda Rogers Associates: 37, 44-45, 56, 66, 67, 70-71, 77, 116-117, 120-121, 124-125, 129, 132, 138-139, 140-141, 146-147, 148-149, 152.
Susan Neale: 190-194, 199, 202-203, 212.
Ewing Paddock: 6, 32, 58, 84, 188, 214.
Tony Payne: 142-143, 144-145, 150, 154-155, 216-221, 229, 231, 234-235, 238-239.
Cynthia Pow: 204-205, 207.
Gary Rees/Linda Rogers Associates: 240-265.
Barry Rowe: 8-31, 86-109.
Joanna Stubbs/B L Kearley Ltd: 113, 114-115, 117, 123, 126, 131, 135.
John Woodcock/Linda Rogers Associates: 196, 200, 206, 208-209.
We thank Heinz Public Relations for their assistance in supplying references for pages 44-45.
KLM Royal Dutch Airlines provided artwork references for pages 242 and 243.

Photographs
Aerofilms Ltd: 128, 244.
All-Sport: 20.
Mohamad Amin/Camerapix: 69.
Heather Angel: 177T.
The Art and Architecture Collection: 77.
Barnaby's Picture Library: 155.
Biofotos: 201L.
Biofotos/Heather Angel: 151.
Biofotos/Brian Rogers: 158L.
Nick Birch: 89, 107R.
BPCC-Aldus Archive: 164, 177B.
BPCC-Aldus Archive/Les Requins Associés (Neuilly): 160R.
British Museum: 12.
British Tourist Authority: 168, 181B, 248T.
Camera Press: 81, 156R.
J Allen Cash Ltd: 100T, 106.
Bruce Coleman Ltd/World Wildlife Fund: 213.
Colorsport: 13.
Daily Telegraph Colour Library: 160L, 182, 260L.
Daily Telegraph Colour Library/Shaun Kelly: 53R, 118.
El Paso Centennial Museum: 14.
Fotofass: 109.
Fotomass Index: 116.
Burt Glinn/Magnum from John Hillelson Agency: 102-103.
Henry Grant: 67.
Ray Green: 50.
susan Griggs Agency: 96.
Richard and Sally Greenhill: 43, 52L, 53, 55, 56, 57, 73, 76, 82, 248BL.
Robert Harding Picture Library: 35T, 39, 80T, 91.
Alan Hutchinson Library: 34-35, 36, 48-49B, 49, 50-51, 51, 52R, 54L, 63R, 79, 88, 94, 105R, 210.
Institute of Geographical Sciences: 154T, 154B.
Frank Lane Agency: 201R, 210-211, 224.

Macdonald & Co/Maggie Murray: 200.
Macdonald & Co/Nick Birch: 107L.
Mansell Collection: 115.
John Massey-Stewart: 252-253.
NASA: 216, 233, 237, 240.
Nissan Motor Company: 127.
Orion Press/Tanio Fuse: 90.
Bury Peerless: 255.
Photographers Library: 176.
Photri: 9, 149.
R K Pilsbury: 221.
Popperfoto: 158-159, 181T, 227B.
Portsmouth City Museum: 186-187.
Rex Features: 78L, 80B, 100B, 104L.
Rex Features/Sipra Press: 264-265.
Alistair Ross: 134.
Royal National Institute for the Blind: 18-19.
Royal National Orthopaedic Hospital: 16.
J Sainsbury plc: 130.
St Bartholomew's Hospital: 19.
Seaphot: 174, 186.
Shell: 185T.
Spectrum Colour Library: 194-195, 197, 198, 206.
Tony Stone Associates: 169, 171, 195, 211.
Homer Sykes: 113.
John Topham Picture Library/Fotogram: 48-49T, 63L.
Varley Picture Agency: 101.
Mireille Vautier: 262.
Vision International/Anthea Sieveking: 34, 90.
ZEFA: 37, 42, 54R, 78R, 83, 112, 122, 123, 138-139, 150-151, 153, 156L, 157, 159, 161, 184, 185B, 199, 205, 219, 225, 227T, 230, 250R&L, 256, 259T&B, 260-261.